PERFECT QUESTIONS PERFECT ANSWERS

BOOKS by
His Divine Grace
A. C. Bhaktivedanta Swami Prabhupāda

Bhagavad-gītā As It Is
Śrīmad-Bhāgavatam, cantos 1-10 (12 vols.)
Śrī Caitanya-caritāmṛta (17 vols.)
Teachings of Lord Caitanya
The Nectar of Devotion
The Nectar of Instruction
Śrī Īśopaniṣad
Easy Journey to Other Planets
Kṛṣṇa Consciousness: The Topmost Yoga System
Kṛṣṇa, The Supreme Personality of Godhead
Perfect Questions, Perfect Answers
Teachings of Lord Kapila, the Son of Devahūti
Transcendental Teachings of Prahlāda Mahārāja
Teachings of Queen Kuntī
Kṛṣṇa, the Reservoir of Pleasure
The Science of Self-Realization
The Path of Perfection
Search for Liberation
The Journey of Self-Discovery
A Second Chance
Laws of Nature
Message of Godhead
Civilization and Transcendence
Life Comes From Life
The Perfection of Yoga
Beyond Birth and Death
On the Way to Kṛṣṇa
Rāja-vidyā: The King of Knowledge
Elevation to Kṛṣṇa Consciousness
Kṛṣṇa Consciousness: The Matchless Gift
Back to Godhead magazine (founder)

available from

The Bhaktivedanta Book Trust
P.O. Box 324, Borehamwood
Herts. WD6 1NB, England
Telephone: 081-905 1244

The Bhaktivedanta Book Trust
3764 Watseka Avenue
Los Angeles, California 90034
USA

The Bhaktivedanta Book Trust
P.O. Box 262
Botany, N.S.W. 2019
Australia

PERFECT QUESTIONS PERFECT ANSWERS

Conversations Between
His Divine Grace
A. C. Bhaktivedanta
Swami Prabhupāda
and Bob Cohen,
a Peace Corps worker
in India

THE BHAKTIVEDANTA BOOK TRUST

Readers interested in the subject matter of this book are invited by the International Society for Krishna Consciousness to visit any ISKCON center worldwide (see address list in back of book) or to correspond with the secretary:

International Society for Krishna Consciousness
P.O. Box 324, Borehamwood, Herts,
WD6 1NB U.K.

International Society for Krishna Consciousness
3764 Watseka Avenue
Los Angeles, California 90034 USA

International Society for Krishna Consciousness
P.O. Box 159, Kings Cross
N.S.W. 2011 Australia

1993 Edition: 220,000 copies

Printed in Germany

ISBN 91-7149-170-8

Contents

Introduction — *ix*

One
The Perfect Science
February 27, 1972 — 1

Two
Material Attachment
February 28, 1972 — 12

Three
Perfect Knowledge
February 28, 1972 (continued) — 17

Four
The Three Modes of Nature
February 28, 1972 (continued) — 25

Five
Becoming Pure
February 29, 1972 — 30

Six
Spiritual Discipline
February 29, 1972 (evening) — 38

Seven
Acting in Knowledge of Kṛṣṇa
February 29, 1972 (evening, continued) — 52

Eight
Advancing in Kṛṣṇa Consciousness
(an exchange of letters) 65

Nine
Deciding for the Future
New York — July 4, 1972 68

Concluding Words 74

His Divine Grace A.C. Bhaktivedanta Swami Prabhupāda 77
Glossary 81
Centres of the International Society for Krishna Consciousness 85
An Introduction to ISKCON and Devotee Life 91

His Divine Grace
A. C. Bhaktivedanta Swami Prabhupāda
Founder-*Ācārya* of the International Society for Krishna Consciousness

Introduction

God, spiritual life — those were such vague terms to me before I met Śrīla Prabhupāda. I have always been interested in religion, but before I met the Hare Kṛṣṇa devotees I somehow did not have the proper perspective needed to enquire fruitfully about spiritual life. The existence of a Creator is only common sense. But who is God? Who am I? I had been to Hebrew School and I had studied Oriental philosophy, but I could never get satisfying answers to my questions.

I first heard the Hare Kṛṣṇa mantra in Greenwich Village, New York, in late 1968:

hare kṛṣṇa hare kṛṣṇa
kṛṣṇa kṛṣṇa hare hare
hare rāma hare rāma
rāma rāma hare hare

The chanting was captivating, and it made me feel very comfortable. The mantra stuck in my mind, and I soon regretted that I had not taken a magazine from the devotees. As explained to me later, a transcendental seed had been planted that could eventually ripen into love of Godhead.

Several months later, I came across a card with the Hare Kṛṣṇa mantra on it. The card promised, "Chant these names of God, and your life will be sublime!" I would occasionally chant, and I found that the mantra did, in fact, give me a feeling of peace of mind.

After graduating from college with a B.S. in Chemistry in 1971, I joined the Peace Corps and went to India as a science teacher. In India I enquired about the Hare Kṛṣṇa movement. I was attracted by the chanting and intrigued by the philosophy, and I was curious about the movement's authenticity. I had visited the Kṛṣṇa temple in New York several times before going to India, but I did not consider the seemingly austere life of a devotee for myself.

I first met the Kṛṣṇa devotees in India at a festival they were holding in Calcutta during October of 1971. The devotees explained to me the purpose of *yoga* and the need to enquire about spiritual life. I began to feel that the rituals and ceremonies they practised were not dull, sentimental obligations, but a real, sensible way of life.

At first, however, it was very difficult for me to understand the philosophy of Kṛṣṇa consciousness. In so many subtle ways, my Western upbringing prevented me from seeing things that were as plain as the nose on my face! Fortunately the devotees convinced me of the need to practise some few basic austerities, and in this way I began to gain some insight into spiritual life. I can now recall how distant and tenuous were my concepts of spirituality and transcendental existence. I met Śrīla Prabhupāda briefly in November of 1971, and shortly thereafter decided to become a vegetarian. (I was proud of being a vegetarian, but later Śrīla Prabhupāda reminded me that even pigeons are, too.)

In February of 1972, I met some devotees in Calcutta who invited me to a festival in Māyāpur (a holy island ninety miles to the north). The festival was to be held in honour of

Lord Caitanya Mahāprabhu, who is considered an incarnation of Kṛṣṇa Himself. I had been planning a trip to Nepal, but the Peace Corps denied me permission to leave India, and so I went to Māyāpur.

I left for Māyāpur planning to stay for two days at the most, but I ended up staying a week. I was the only Western nondevotee on the island, and since I was living with the devotees on their land, this was a unique opportunity to learn intimately about Kṛṣṇa consciousness.

On the third day of the festival I was invited in to see Śrīla Prabhupāda. He was living in a small, half-brick and half-thatched hut, with two or three pieces of simple furniture. Śrīla Prabhupāda asked me to be seated, and then asked how I was and whether I had any questions. The devotees had explained to me that Śrīla Prabhupāda could answer my questions because he represents a disciplic succession of spiritual masters. I thought that Śrīla Prabhupāda might really know what is going on in the world. After all, his devotees claimed this, and I admired and respected them. So with this in mind I began to ask my questions. Inadvertently, I had approached a *guru*, or spiritual master, in the prescribed way — by submissively asking questions about spiritual life.

Śrīla Prabhupāda seemed pleased with me, and over the next several days he answered my questions. I asked them mostly from an academic point of view, but he always gave me personal answers so that I would actually spiritualise my life. His answers were logical, scientific, satisfying and amazingly lucid. Before I met Śrīla Prabhupāda and his disciples, spiritual life was always obscure and nebulous. But the discussions with Śrīla Prabhupāda were realistic, clear and exciting! Śrīla Prabhupāda was patiently trying to help me understand that Kṛṣṇa, God, is the supreme enjoyer,

supreme friend and supreme proprietor. I put forward many impediments to accepting the obvious: that I would have to become serious about God consciousness to understand God. But Śrīla Prabhupāda relentlessly, yet kindly, urged me on. Even though I had little ability to express myself, Śrīla Prabhupāda understood my every enquiry and answered perfectly.

Bob Cohen
August 14, 1974

ONE

The Perfect Science
February 27, 1972

Śrīla Prabhupāda: Kṛṣṇa means "all-attractive". So unless God is all-attractive, how can He be God? A man is important when he is attractive. Is it not?
Bob: It is so.
Śrīla Prabhupāda: So, God must be attractive, and attractive for all. Therefore, if God has any name, or if you want to give any name to God, only "Kṛṣṇa" can be given.
Bob: Why only the name Kṛṣṇa?
Śrīla Prabhupāda: Because He's all-attractive; Kṛṣṇa means "all-attractive". God has no name, but by His qualities we give Him names. If a man is very beautiful, we call him "beautiful". If a man is very intelligent, we call him "wise". So the name is given according to the quality. Because God is all-attractive, the name Kṛṣṇa can be applied only to Him. Kṛṣṇa means "all-attractive". It includes everything.
Bob: What about a name meaning "all-powerful"?
Śrīla Prabhupāda: Yes, unless you are powerful, how can you be all-attractive? God must be very beautiful; He must be very wise; He must be very powerful; He must be very famous.
Bob: Is Kṛṣṇa attractive to rascals?
Śrīla Prabhupāda: Oh, yes! He was the greatest rascal also.
Bob: How is that?

Śrīla Prabhupāda: Because He was always teasing the *gopīs*. Sometimes when Rādhārāṇī [Kṛṣṇa's divine consort] would go out, Kṛṣṇa would attack Her. And when She would fall down She would call out, "Kṛṣṇa, don't torture Me in that way." Then Kṛṣṇa would take the opportunity to kiss Her. Rādhārāṇī was very pleased; but superficially Kṛṣṇa was the greatest rascal. So unless rascaldom is in Kṛṣṇa, how can rascaldom exist in the world? Our formula of God is that He is the source of everything. Unless rascaldom is in Kṛṣṇa, how can it be manifest? He is the source of everything, but His rascaldom is so nice that everyone worships it.

Bob: What about rascals who aren't nice?

Śrīla Prabhupāda: No, rascaldom is not nice, but Kṛṣṇa is absolute; He is God. Therefore His rascaldom is also good. Kṛṣṇa is all-good. God is good. Therefore, when He becomes a rascal, that is also good. That is Kṛṣṇa. Rascaldom is not good, but when it is practised by Kṛṣṇa, because He is absolutely good, that rascaldom is also good. One has to understand this.

Bob: Are there some people who do not find Kṛṣṇa attractive?

Śrīla Prabhupāda: No. All people will find Him attractive. Who is not attracted? Just give an example: "This man or this living entity is not attracted to Kṛṣṇa." Just find such a person.

Bob: Somebody who wishes to do things in life that he may feel are wrong, but who wishes to gain power or prestige or money, may find God unattractive. He may not find God attractive, because God gives him guilt.

Śrīla Prabhupāda: No, God does not make him feel guilty. The man is attracted to becoming powerful. He wants to become powerful or rich — is it not? But nobody is richer than Kṛṣṇa; therefore Kṛṣṇa is attractive to him.

Bob: If a person who wants to become rich prays to Kṛṣṇa, will he become rich?
Śrīla Prabhupāda: Oh, yes!
Bob: Can he become rich this way?
Śrīla Prabhupāda: Oh, yes. Because Kṛṣṇa is all-powerful, if you pray to Him to become rich, Kṛṣṇa will make you rich.
Bob: If somebody lives an evil life but prays to become rich, will he still become rich?
Śrīla Prabhupāda: Yes. Praying to Kṛṣṇa is not evil. Somehow or other he prays to Kṛṣṇa, so you cannot say that he is evil.
Bob: Oh yes.
Śrīla Prabhupāda: Kṛṣṇa says in *Bhagavad-gītā, api cet su-durācāro bhajate mām ananya-bhāk.* Have you read it?
Bob: Yes. I don't know the Sanskrit, but the English I do: "Even if the most evil man prays to Me he will be elevated."
Śrīla Prabhupāda: Yes. As soon as he begins to pray to Kṛṣṇa, that is not evil. Therefore Kṛṣṇa is all-attractive. It is said in the *Vedas* that the Absolute Truth, or the Supreme Personality of Godhead, is the reservoir of all pleasure: *raso vai saḥ.* Everyone is hankering after something because he relishes some mellow in it.
Bob: Excuse me?
Śrīla Prabhupāda: Some mellow. Suppose a man is drinking. Why is he drinking? He is getting some mellow out of that drinking. A man is hankering after money because by possessing money he gets a mellow out of it.
Bob: What does mellow mean?
Śrīla Prabhupāda: Pleasing taste. So the *Vedas* say, *raso vai saḥ.* The exact translation of mellow is *rasa.* [*Mālatī, the wife of Prabhupāda's secretary, enters with a tray of food*] What is that?
Mālatī: Eggplant, fried.

Śrīla Prabhupāda: Oh! All-attractive! All-attractive!

* * *

Bob: Thank you so much for allowing me to ask my questions.
Śrīla Prabhupāda: That is my mission. People should understand the science of God. Unless we cooperate with the Supreme Lord, our life is baffled. I have given the example many times that a screw which has fallen from a machine has no value. But when the same screw is again attached to the machine, it has value. Similarly, we are part and parcel of God. So without God, what is our value? No value! We should again come back to our position of attachment to God. Then we have value.
Bob: What is a scientist?
Śrīla Prabhupāda: One who knows things as they are.
Bob: He thinks he knows things as they are. Hopes he knows things as they are.
Śrīla Prabhupāda: No. He is supposed to know. We approach the scientist because he is supposed to know things correctly. A scientist means one who knows things as they are.
Śyāmasundara [*Śrīla Prabhupāda's secretary*]: How is Kṛṣṇa the greatest scientist?
Śrīla Prabhupāda: Because He knows everything. A scientist is one who knows a subject matter thoroughly. He is a scientist, and Kṛṣṇa knows everything.
Bob: I am a science teacher.
Śrīla Prabhupāda: Yes, but unless you have perfect knowledge, how can you teach? That is our question.
Bob: Without perfect knowledge you can teach —
Śrīla Prabhupāda: That is cheating; that is not teaching. That

is cheating. Just like the scientists say, "There was a chunk and the creation took place. Perhaps. Maybe." What is this? Simply cheating! It is not teaching; it is cheating.

Bob: Without perfect knowledge, can I not teach some things?

Śrīla Prabhupāda: You can teach up to the point you know.

Bob: Yes, but I should not claim to teach more than I know.

Śrīla Prabhupāda: Yes, that is cheating.

Śyāmasundara: In other words, he can't teach the truth with partial knowledge.

Śrīla Prabhupāda: Yes. That is not possible for any human being. A human being has imperfect senses, so how can he teach perfect knowledge? Suppose you see the sun as a disc. You have no means to approach the sun. If you say that we can see the sun by telescope, which is also made by you, who are imperfect, then how can your machine be perfect? Therefore, your knowledge of the sun is imperfect. So don't teach about the sun unless you have perfect knowledge. That is cheating.

Bob: But what about teaching that the sun is supposedly 93,000,000 miles away?

Śrīla Prabhupāda: As soon as you say "it is supposed", that is not scientific.

Bob: But I think that almost all science, then, is not scientific.

Śrīla Prabhupāda: That is the point!

Bob: All science is based on suppositions of one kind or another.

Śrīla Prabhupāda: Yes. They are teaching imperfectly. Just like they are advertising so much about the moon. Do you think their knowledge is perfect?

Bob: No.

Śrīla Prabhupāda: Then?

Bob: So what is the proper duty of a teacher in society? Let us say a science teacher. What should I be doing in the classroom?
Śrīla Prabhupāda: You should simply teach about Kṛṣṇa. That will include everything. Your aim should be to know Kṛṣṇa.
Bob: Can a scientist teach the science of combining acid and alkaline — science with Kṛṣṇa as its object?
Śrīla Prabhupāda: How can it be?
Bob: When we study science, we find general tendencies of nature. These general tendencies of nature point to a controlling force.
Śrīla Prabhupāda: I was explaining that the other day. I asked a chemist whether, according to chemical formulas, hydrogen and oxygen linked together become water. Do they not?
Bob: It's true.
Śrīla Prabhupāda: Now, there is a vast amount of water in the Atlantic Ocean and the Pacific Ocean. What quantity of chemicals was required? How many tons?
Bob: Many!
Śrīla Prabhupāda: Somebody must have supplied it. So who supplied it?
Bob: This was supplied by God.
Śrīla Prabhupāda: Somebody must have supplied it.
Bob: Yes.
Śrīla Prabhupāda: So that is science. You can teach like that.
Bob: Should one bother teaching about acid and alkaline combining to form a neutral?
Śrīla Prabhupāda: That is the same thing. Who is supplying the acid and alkaline?
Bob: They come from the same source as the water.
Śrīla Prabhupāda: Yes. You cannot manufacture water

unless you have hydrogen and oxygen. So there are millions of planets, and there are millions of Atlantic and Pacific oceans. Who created this water with hydrogen and oxygen, and how was it supplied? That is our question. Somebody must have supplied it; otherwise, how has it come into existence?

Bob: But should the procedure of burning hydrogen and oxygen together to make water also be taught?

Śrīla Prabhupāda: That is secondary, not very difficult. Just like Mālatī made this *purī* [a kind of bread]. So there is flour and there is ghee [clarified butter], and she made a *purī.* But unless there is ghee and flour, where is the chance of making a *purī*? In the *Bhagavad-gītā* Kṛṣṇa states: "Water, earth, air, fire — they are My energies." What is your body? It is your energy. Do you know that? Your body is made out of your energy. For example, I am eating, so I am creating some energy, and therefore my body is maintained. So therefore my body is made out of my energy.

Bob: When you eat, there is energy from the sun in the food.

Śrīla Prabhupāda: I am creating some energy by digesting the food, and that is maintaining my body. If your energy supply is not proper, then your body becomes weak or unhealthy; your body is made out of your own energy. Similarly, this gigantic cosmic body — the universe — is made of Kṛṣṇa's energy. How can you deny it? As your body is made out of your energy, similarly the universal body must be made out of somebody's energy. That is Kṛṣṇa.

Bob: I'll have to think about that to follow that point.

Śrīla Prabhupāda: What is there to follow? It is a fact. Your hair is growing daily. Why? Because you have some energy.

Bob: I obtain the energy from my food.

Śrīla Prabhupāda: Somehow or other you have obtained that energy, and through it your hair is growing. Just as your body is manufactured by your energy, similarly the whole gigantic manifestation is made of God's energy — not *your* energy. That is a fact.

Bob: Yes, I see that. Aren't the planets in this universe a product of the sun's energy?

Śrīla Prabhupāda: Yes. But who produced the sun? That is Kṛṣṇa's energy. Because it is heat, and Kṛṣṇa says, *bhūmir āpo 'nalo vāyuḥ:* "Heat — that is My energy." Therefore the sun is the representation of the heating energy of Kṛṣṇa. It is not your energy. You cannot say, "The sun is made by me." But somebody must have made it, and Kṛṣṇa says that He did. So, we believe Kṛṣṇa. Therefore we are Kṛṣṇa-ites.

Bob: Kṛṣṇa-ites?

Śrīla Prabhupāda: Yes. If I say that heat is the energy of Kṛṣṇa, you cannot deny it, because it is not your energy. In your body there is a certain amount of heat. Heat is someone's energy. And who is that person? That is Kṛṣṇa. And Kṛṣṇa says, "Yes, it is My energy. This earth, water, fire, air, ether, mind, intelligence and ego — they are My eight separated energies." So my knowledge is perfect. I may be a fool personally, but because I take knowledge from the greatest scientist, I am the greatest scientist.

Bob: Why are they *separated* energies?

Śrīla Prabhupāda: Just like this milk. What is this milk? The separated energy of the cow, is it not?

Bob: But what is the significance of this energy being separated from Kṛṣṇa?

Śrīla Prabhupāda: "Separated" means that this milk is made out of the body of the cow, but it is not the cow. That is separation.

Bob: So, this earth is made out of Kṛṣṇa, but it is not Kṛṣṇa?

Śrīla Prabhupāda: It is not Kṛṣṇa. Or, you can say, Kṛṣṇa and not Kṛṣṇa simultaneously. That is our philosophy. One and different. You cannot say that these things are different from Kṛṣṇa, because without Kṛṣṇa they have no existence. At the same time, you cannot say, "Then let me worship water. Why worship Kṛṣṇa? The pantheists say that because everything is God, whatever we do is God worship. This is *Māyāvāda* philosophy — that because everything is made of God, therefore everything is God. But our philosophy is that everything is God, but also not God.

Bob: Is there anything on earth that is God?

Śrīla Prabhupāda: Yes. Because everything is made out of the energy of God. But that does not mean that by worshipping everything you are worshipping God.

Bob: So what is on earth that is not *māyā*?

Śrīla Prabhupāda: *Māyā* means "energy".

Bob: It means energy? I thought it meant illusion.

Śrīla Prabhupāda: Yes, another meaning of *māyā* is "illusion". So foolish people accept the energy as the energetic. That is *māyā*. Just like sunshine: it enters your room, and it is the energy of the sun. But because the sunshine enters your room, you cannot say that the sun has entered. If the sun enters your room, then your room and yourself — everything — will be finished. Immediately. You will not have the leisure to understand that the sun has entered. Is it not?

Bob: It is so.

Śrīla Prabhupāda: But without the sun, where is the sunshine? So you cannot say that sunshine is not the sun. Yet at the same time, it is not the sun. It is both the sun and not the sun. That is our philosophy: *acintya-bhedābheda* — inconceivable. In the material sense, you cannot conceive that a thing is simultaneously positive and negative. That is inconceivable energy. And because everything is Kṛṣṇa's energy, Kṛṣṇa can manifest Himself through any energy. Therefore, when we worship Kṛṣṇa in a form made of earth, water, or something like that, that is Kṛṣṇa. You cannot say that it is not Kṛṣṇa. When we worship this metal Deity form of Kṛṣṇa in the temple, that is Kṛṣṇa. That's a fact, because metal is an energy of Kṛṣṇa; therefore, it is nondifferent from Kṛṣṇa. And Kṛṣṇa is so powerful that He can present Himself fully in His energy. So this Deity worship is not heathenism. It is actually worship of God, provided you know the process.

Bob: If you know the process, then the Deity becomes Kṛṣṇa?

Śrīla Prabhupāda: Not becomes — it *is* Kṛṣṇa.

Bob: The Deity is Kṛṣṇa, but only if you know the process.

Śrīla Prabhupāda: Yes. Just like this electronic wire — it is electricity. One who knows the process can derive electricity out of it. Otherwise it is just wire.

Bob: So if I build a statue of Kṛṣṇa, it is not Kṛṣṇa unless —

Śrīla Prabhupāda: It is Kṛṣṇa. But you have to know the process of understanding that it is Kṛṣṇa. It is Kṛṣṇa.

Bob: It is not just earth and mud.

Śrīla Prabhupāda: No. Earth has no separate existence without Kṛṣṇa. Kṛṣṇa says, "My energy." You cannot separate the energy from the energetic, that is not possible. You cannot separate heat from fire. But fire is different from the heat, and heat is different from the fire. You are taking heat; that does not mean you are touching fire. Fire, in spite of emanating heat, keeps its identity.

Similarly, although Kṛṣṇa, by His different energies, is creating everything, He remains Kṛṣṇa. The Māyāvādī philosophers think that if Kṛṣṇa is everything, then Kṛṣṇa's separate identity is lost. That is material thinking. For example, by drinking this milk, little by little, when I finish there is no more milk; it has gone to my belly. Kṛṣṇa is not like that. He is omnipotent. We are utilising His energy continually; still He is there, present.

A crude example: a man begets children unlimitedly, but the man is still there. It's not that because he has produced hundreds of children, he is finished. So, similarly, God or Kṛṣṇa, in spite of His unlimited number of children, is there. *Pūrṇasya pūrṇam ādāya pūrṇam evāvaśiṣyate:* "Because He is the complete whole, even though so many complete units emanate from Him, He remains the complete balance." This is Kṛṣṇa consciousness. Kṛṣṇa is never finished; He is so powerful. Therefore He is all-attractive. This is one side of the display of Kṛṣṇa's energy. Similarly, He has unlimited energies. This study of Kṛṣṇa's energy is only one side, one portion. So in this way, if you go on studying Kṛṣṇa, that is Kṛṣṇa consciousness. It is not a "maybe", "perhaps not". Absolutely! It is!

Śyāmasundara: And the study itself is never finished.

Śrīla Prabhupāda: No. How can it be? Kṛṣṇa has unlimited energy.

TWO

Material Attachment
February 28, 1972

Bob: I've asked devotees about sex in their relationships. And although I see the way they feel, I can't see myself acting the same way. See, I'll be getting married at the end of the summer, in September or August when I return to America. The devotees have told me that householders have sex only to conceive a child. I cannot picture myself following that. So what kind of sex life can a devotee lead living in the material world?

Śrīla Prabhupāda: The Vedic principle is that one should avoid sex life altogether. The whole Vedic principle is to get liberation from material bondage. There are different attachments for material enjoyment, of which sex life is the topmost enjoyment. The *Bhāgavatam* says that in this material world *puṁsaḥ striyā mithunī-bhāvam etam:* "Man is attached to woman, and woman is attached to man." Not only in human society, in animal society also. That attachment is the basic principle of material life. So a woman is hankering after the association of a man, and a man is seeking the association of a woman. All the fiction novels, dramas, cinema and even ordinary advertisements that you see simply depict the attachment between man and woman. Even in the department store you will find some woman and man in the window. *Pravṛttir eṣā bhūtānāṁ nivṛttis tu* *mahāphalām.* ["Everyone in material life is attracted to furthering the way of attachment, but the greatest treasure is to be gained by following the path of detachment."] So this attachment is already there.

Bob: Attachment between man and woman?

Śrīla Prabhupāda: Man and woman. So if you want to get liberation from this material world, then that attachment should be reduced to nil. Otherwise, simply further attachment. You will have to take rebirth, either as a human being, or as a demigod, or as an animal such as a serpent, a bird or a beast. You will have to take birth. So this basic principle of increasing attachment is not our business, although it is the general tendency. *Gṛha, kṣetra, suta:* home, land, sons. But if one can reduce and stop it, that is first-class. Therefore our Vedic system is to first of all train a boy as a *brahmacārī:* no sex life. The Vedic principle is to reduce attachment, not to increase it. The Indian system calls for *varṇa* and *āśrama:* four social orders and four spiritual orders. *Brahmacarya,* or celibate student life, *gṛhastha,* or married life, *vānaprastha,* or retired life and *sannyāsa,* renounced life. These are the spiritual orders. And the social orders are *brāhmaṇas,* or teachers, *kṣatriyas,* or administrators, *vaiśyas,* or merchants and farmers and *śūdras,* or ordinary workers. Therefore the whole system is called *varṇāśrama-dharma.* So under this system, the regulative principles are so nice that even if one has the tendency to enjoy material life, he is so nicely moulded that at last he achieves liberation and goes back home, back to Godhead. This is the process. So sex life is not required; but because we are attached to it there are some regulative principles under which it is maintained. It is said in *Śrīmad-Bhāgavatam:*

puṁsaḥ striyā mithunī-bhāvam etaṁ
tayor mitho hṛdaya-granthim āhuḥ

ato gṛha-kṣetra-sutāpta-vittair
janasya moho 'yam ahaṁ mameti

This sex life, attachment for man or woman, is the basic principle of material life. And when a man and woman are united, that attachment becomes increased. And that increased attachment induces one to accumulate *gṛha* (a home), *kṣetra* (land), *suta* (children), *āpta* (friendship or society) and *vitta* (money). In this way — *gṛha-kṣetra-sutāpta-vittaiḥ* — he becomes entangled. *Janasya moho 'yam:* this is the illusion. And by this illusion he thinks, *ahaṁ mameti:* "I am this body, and anything in relationship with this body is mine."

Material attachment involves thinking, "I am this body, and because I have this body in a particular place, that is my country." And that is going on: "I am American. I am Indian. I am German. I am this or that. I am this body. This is my country, and I shall sacrifice everything for my country and society." So in this way, the illusion increases. And under this illusion, he gets another body when he dies. That may be a superior body or an inferior body, according to his *karma.* Yet even if he gets a superior body or goes to the heavenly planets, that is also an entanglement. There is even every chance of becoming a cat or a dog or a tree. This science is not known in the world: how the soul is transmigrating from one body to another, and how he is being entrapped in different types of bodies. This science is unknown. In the *Bhagavad-gītā* Arjuna lamented, "How can I kill my brother, or my grandfather on the other side?" Yet his thinking was simply on the basis of the bodily concept of life. When his problems could not be solved, he surrendered to Kṛṣṇa and accepted Him as spiritual master. And when Kṛṣṇa became his spiritual master, Kṛṣṇa chastised Arjuna:

aśocyān anvaśocas tvaṁ
prajñā-vādāṁś ca bhāṣase
gatāsūn agatāsūṁś ca
nānuśocanti paṇḍitāḥ

"You are talking like a learned man, but you are fool number one because you are talking about the bodily concept of life." So because sex life increases the bodily concept of life, the whole process is to reduce it to nil.

Bob: To reduce it over the stages of your life?

Śrīla Prabhupāda: Yes. Reduce it. A boy is trained as a *brahmacārī* student up to twenty-five years, restricting sex life. So, some of the boys remain *naiṣṭhika-brahmacārī*, or celibate for life. Because they are given education to become fully conversant with spiritual knowledge, they don't want to marry. In Vedic society even within marriage there is regulation, but the principle is that one cannot have sex life without being married.

In human society there is marriage, not in animal society. But people are gradually descending from human society to animal society. They are forgetting marriage. That is also predicted in the *śāstras* [scriptures]. *Dāmpatye 'bhirucir hetuḥ:* in the Kali-yuga (the present age), there will eventually be no marriage performances; the boy and the girl will simply agree to live together, and their relationship will be based upon sexual power. And if the man or the woman becomes deficient in sex life, then there is divorce. So, for this philosophy many Western philosophers like Freud and others have written so many books.

But according to Vedic culture, we are interested in sex only for begetting children, that's all — not to study the psychology of sex life. There is already natural psychology for that. Even if one does not read any philosophy, he is sexually inclined. Nobody is taught it in the schools and colleges. Everyone already knows how to do it. That is the general tendency. But education should be given to stop it. That is real education.

Bob: In America at present that's a radical concept.

Śrīla Prabhupāda: Well, in America there are so many things requiring reformation, and the Kṛṣṇa consciousness movement will bring that. I went to your country and saw that the boys and girls were living like friends, so I told my students, "You cannot live together as friends; you must get yourselves married."

Bob: Many people see that even marriage is not sacred, so they find no desire to marry. Because people get married, and if things are not proper, they get a divorce so very easily. Therefore some people feel that to get married is not meaningful.

Śrīla Prabhupāda: No, their idea is that marriage is for legalised prostitution. They think like that, but that is not marriage. Even the Christian paper *Watchtower* has criticised a priest who allowed a marriage between two men, homosexuality. So these things are all going on. They take it purely for prostitution, that's all. So therefore people are thinking, "What is the use of keeping a regular prostitute at such heavy expenditure? Better not to have this." When the milk is available in the marketplace, what is the use of keeping a cow? It is a very abominable condition in the Western countries. I have seen it. Here also in India, it is gradually coming. Therefore we have started this Kṛṣṇa consciousness movement to educate people in the essential principles of spiritual life. It is not a sectarian religious movement. It is a cultural movement for everyone's benefit.

THREE

Perfect Knowledge
February 28, 1972
(continued)

Śrīla Prabhupāda: This movement is especially meant to enable a human being to reach the real goal of life.
Bob: Is the real goal of life to know God?
Śrīla Prabhupāda: Yes. To go back home, back to Godhead. That is the real goal of life. The water that comes from the sea forms clouds: the clouds fall down as rain. The water's actual goal is to flow down the river and again enter the sea. So, we have come from God, and now we are embarrassed by material life. Therefore, our aim should be to get out of this embarrassing situation and go back home, back to Godhead. This is the real goal of life.

mām upetya punar janma
duḥkhālayam aśāśvatam
nāpnuvanti mahātmānaḥ
saṁsiddhiṁ paramāṁ gatāḥ

That is the version of *Bhagavad-gītā*. "If anyone comes to Me" — *mām upetya* — "he does not come back again." Come back to where? To this place, *duḥkhālayam aśāśvatam.* This place is the abode of miseries. Everyone knows, but they have been befooled by so-called leaders. Material life is miserable life. Kṛṣṇa, God, says that this place is *duḥkhālayam,* a place of miseries. And it is also *aśāśvatam,* temporary.

You cannot make a compromise: "All right, let it be miserable. I shall remain here as an American or Indian." No. That also you cannot do. You cannot remain an American. You may think that, having been born in America, you are very happy. But you cannot remain an American for long. You will have to be kicked out of that place, and your next life you do not know. Therefore, it is *duḥkhālayam aśāśvatam* — miserable and temporary. That is our philosophy.

Bob: Is life not so miserable if you have some knowledge of God?

Śrīla Prabhupāda: No! *Some* knowledge will not do. You must have perfect knowledge. *Janma karma ca me divyam evaṁ yo vetti tattvataḥ. Tattvatah* means "perfectly". Perfect knowledge is being taught in *Bhagavad-gītā.* So we are giving everyone in human society a chance to learn *Bhagavad-gītā* as it is and make his life perfect. That is the Kṛṣṇa consciousness movement. What does your science say about the transmigration of the soul?

Bob: I think that science cannot deny or affirm it. Science does not know it.

Śrīla Prabhupāda: Therefore I say that science is imperfect.

Bob: Science though, may say something. It says that energy is never destroyed; it is changed.

Śrīla Prabhupāda: That's all right. But how the energy is working in the future, that science does not know. How is the energy transmuted? How, by different manipulations, is the energy working differently? For instance, by different handling electrical energy is operating the heating and the refrigerator. They are opposites, but the electrical energy is the same. Similarly, this energy — living energy — how is it being directed? Which way is it going? How is it fructifying in the next life? That they do not know. But in *Bhagavad-gītā* it is very simply stated, *vāsāṁsi jīrṇāni yathā vihāya:* You are covered by a dress, by a shirt. When this shirt is unusable, you change it. Similarly, this body is just like a shirt and coat. When it is no longer workable, we have to change it.

Bob: What is the "we" that has to change? What is constant?

Śrīla Prabhupāda: That is the soul.

Bob: From one life to the next?

Śrīla Prabhupāda: That is the soul: I. What "you" is speaking? You! What "I" is speaking? Identity: *ātmā*, or soul.

Bob: My soul is different from your soul?

Śrīla Prabhupāda: Yes. You are an individual soul; I am an individual soul.

Bob: You have removed yourself from karmic influences. If I was to remove myself from karmic influences, would our souls be the same or different?

Śrīla Prabhupāda: The soul is of the same quality in everyone. You are under a certain conception of life at the present moment, as were these countrymen of yours [*gesturing to the devotees in the room*], but by training they have taken to another conception of life. So the ultimate training is how to become Kṛṣṇa conscious. That is the perfection.

Bob: If two people are Kṛṣṇa conscious, is their soul the same?

Śrīla Prabhupāda: The soul is always the same.

Bob: Is it the same in each person?

Śrīla Prabhupāda: Yes.

Bob: [*pointing to two devotees*] If these two are Kṛṣṇa conscious, are their souls the same?

Śrīla Prabhupāda: The soul is the same but always individual, even if one is not Kṛṣṇa conscious. For instance, you are a human being, and I am a human being. Even if I am not a Christian, even if you are not a Hindu, still we are human beings. Similarly, the soul may not be Kṛṣṇa conscious, or he may be Kṛṣṇa conscious — it doesn't matter. But the soul is the soul.

Bob: Can you tell me more about this?

Śrīla Prabhupāda: Soul. As pure spirit all souls are equal. Even in an animal. Therefore it is said, *paṇḍitāḥ sama-darśinaḥ:* Those who are actually learned do not see the outward covering, either in a human being or in an animal.

Bob: I have considered the soul somewhat as part of God. At times I think I feel God. I'm here, and it may be said that God is here. So if the soul is inside me, then should I be able to feel God inside me? Not all of God, I mean, but a part of God. Although I don't feel God in me, but God may be here, separate from me. But should I be able to feel God inside me, since my soul is part of God?

Śrīla Prabhupāda: Yes. God is inside and outside also. God is everywhere. This is to be known.

Bob: How do you feel God inside you?

Śrīla Prabhupāda: Not in the beginning, but you have to know from the *śāstras,* by the Vedic information. For example, in the *Bhagavad-gītā* it is said, *īśvaraḥ sarva-bhūtānāṁ hṛd-deśe 'rjuna tiṣṭhati:* "God is there in everyone's heart." *Paramāṇu-cayāntara-stham:* "God is also within every atom." So this is the first information. And then, by the yogic process, you have to realise it.

Bob: What kind of yogic process must I do to find out? To feel this information? To feel the soul inside?

Śrīla Prabhupāda: There are many yogic processes. But for this age this process is very nice — chanting Hare Kṛṣṇa.

Bob: Through this I can feel not only God outside but God inside?

Śrīla Prabhupāda: You'll understand everything of God: how

God is inside, how God is outside, how God is working. Everything will be revealed. By this attitude of service, God will reveal Himself. You cannot understand God by your endeavour; only if God reveals Himself. For instance, when the sun is out of your sight at night, you cannot see it by your torchlight, or any light. But in the morning you can see the sun automatically without any torchlight. Similarly, you have to put yourself in a situation in which God will be revealed. It is not that by some method you can ask God, "Please come. I will see You." No, God is not your order-carrier.

Bob: You must please God for Him to reveal Himself. How do we know when we are pleasing God?

Śrīla Prabhupāda: When you see Him, then you will understand. Just as when you eat you do not require to ask anyone whether you are feeling strength or your hunger is satisfied. If you eat, you understand that you are feeling energy. You don't need to enquire from anyone. Similarly, if you actually serve God, then you will understand, "God is dictating to me. God is there. I am seeing God."

Śyāmasundara: Or God's representative.

Śrīla Prabhupāda: Yes. You have to go through God's representative. *Yasya prasādād bhagavat-prasādaḥ:* If you please God's representative, then automatically God becomes pleased, and thus you can directly see Him.

Bob: How can we please God's representative?

Śrīla Prabhupāda: You have to carry out his orders, that's all. God's representative is the guru. He asks you to do this, to do that; if you do it, that is pleasing. *Yasyāprasādān na gatiḥ kuto 'pi:* If you displease him, then you are nowhere. Therefore we worship the guru. *Sākṣād-dharitvena samasta-śāstrair uktas tathā bhāvyata eva sadbhiḥ:* The guru should be accepted as God. That is the injunction of all *śāstra.*

Bob: The guru should be accepted as a representative of God?

Śrīla Prabhupāda: Yes, the guru is God's representative. The guru is the external manifestation of Kṛṣṇa.

Bob: But different from the incarnations of Kṛṣṇa that come?

Śrīla Prabhupāda: Yes.

Bob: In what way is the external manifestation of the guru different from the external manifestation of Kṛṣṇa or Caitanya when They come to earth?

Śrīla Prabhupāda: The guru is the representative of Kṛṣṇa. So there are symptoms of who is a guru. The general symptoms are described in the *Vedas*.

tad-vijñānārthaṁ sa gurum evābhigacchet
samit-pāṇiḥ śrotriyaṁ brahma-niṣṭham

A guru must come in a disciplic succession, and he must have heard thoroughly about the *Vedas* from his spiritual master. Generally a guru's symptom is that he is a perfect devotee, that's all. And he serves Kṛṣṇa by preaching His message.

Bob: Was Lord Caitanya a different type of guru than you are?

Śrīla Prabhupāda: No, no. Gurus cannot be of different types. All gurus are of one type.

Bob: Was Caitanya also an incarnation at the same time?

Śrīla Prabhupāda: Yes, He is Kṛṣṇa Himself, but He is representing the guru. Because Kṛṣṇa was God, He demanded, *sarva-dharmān parityajya mām ekaṁ śaraṇam vraja:* "Abandon all varieties of religion and just surrender unto Me." But people misunderstood Him. Therefore Kṛṣṇa again came as a guru and taught people how to surrender to Kṛṣṇa.

Śyāmasundara: Doesn't Kṛṣṇa say in *Bhagavad-gītā*, "I am the spiritual master"?

Śrīla Prabhupāda: Yes, He is the original spiritual master because He was accepted as spiritual master by Arjuna. *Śiṣyas te 'haṁ śādhi māṁ tvāṁ prapannam.* Arjuna told the Lord, "I am Your disciple, and a soul surrendered unto You. Please instruct me." So unless Kṛṣṇa is a spiritual master, how does Arjuna become His disciple? He is the original guru. *Tene brahma hṛdā ya ādi-kavaye:* "It is Kṛṣṇa only who first imparted Vedic knowledge unto the heart of Brahmā, the first created being." Therefore He is the original guru. Then His disciple, Brahmā, is a guru; then his disciple, Nārada, is a guru; then his disciple, Vyāsa, is a guru. In this way there is a *guru-paramparā,* or disciplic succession of gurus. *Evaṁ paramparā-prāptam:* "The transcendental knowledge is received through the disciplic succession."

Bob: So a guru receives his knowledge through the disciplic succession, not directly from Kṛṣṇa? Do you receive some knowledge directly from Kṛṣṇa?

Śrīla Prabhupāda: Yes. Kṛṣṇa's direct instruction is there: *Bhagavad-gītā.* But you have to learn it through the disciplic succession, otherwise you will misunderstand it.

Bob: But presently you do not receive information directly from Kṛṣṇa? It comes through the disciplic succession from the books?

Śrīla Prabhupāda: There is no difference. Suppose I say that this is a pencil. If you say to someone, "There is a pencil," and if he says to another man, "This is a pencil," then what is the difference between his instruction and my instruction?

Bob: Kṛṣṇa's mercy allows you to know this now?

Śrīla Prabhupāda: You can take Kṛṣṇa's mercy also, provided it is delivered as it is. Just as we are teaching *Bhagavad-gītā.* In *Bhagavad-gītā* Kṛṣṇa says, *sarva-dharmān parityajya mām ekaṁ śaraṇam vraja:* "Just give up all other forms of religion and simply surrender unto Me." Now we are saying that you should give up everything and surrender to Kṛṣṇa. Therefore, there is no difference between Kṛṣṇa's instruction and our instruction; there is no deviation. So if you receive knowledge in that perfect way, that is as good as receiving instruction directly from Kṛṣṇa. But we don't change anything.

Bob: When I pray reverently, faithfully, does Kṛṣṇa hear me?

Śrīla Prabhupāda: Yes.

Bob: From me to Him?

Śrīla Prabhupāda: Yes, because He is within your heart He is always hearing you — whether you are praying or not praying. When you are doing some nonsense, He is also hearing you. And when you pray, that is very welcome.

Bob: To Kṛṣṇa's ear, is praying louder than nonsense?

Śrīla Prabhupāda: No. He is all-perfect; He can hear everything. Even if you don't speak, even if you simply think, "I shall do it," then He hears you. *Sarvasya cāhaṁ hṛdi sanniviṣṭaḥ:* "Kṛṣṇa is seated in everyone's heart."

Bob: And should one pray?

Śrīla Prabhupāda: Yes. Praying is every living entity's only business. *Eko bahūnāṁ yo vidadhāti kāmān.* That is the statement of the *Vedas.* "Kṛṣṇa supplies everything to everyone." He is supplying food to everyone, so He is the Father. So why should you not pray, "Father, give me this"? Just as in the Christian Bible there is, "Father, give us our daily bread." That is good; they are accepting the Supreme Father. But grown-up children should not ask from the father; rather, they should be prepared to serve the father. That is *bhakti,* devotion.

Bob: You solve my questions so nicely.

Śrīla Prabhupāda: Thank you very much.

FOUR

The Three Modes of Nature February 28, 1972 (continued)

Bob: I have read that there are three *guṇas* (passion, ignorance and goodness) in life. Could you explain this somewhat? Especially what is meant by the mode of ignorance and the mode of goodness.

Śrīla Prabhupāda: In goodness you can understand knowledge. You can know that there is God, that this world was created by Him, and so many actual things — the sun is this, the moon is this — perfect knowledge. If one has some knowledge, even though it may not be perfect, that is goodness. In passion one identifies with his material body and tries to gratify his senses. That is passion. Ignorance is animal life. In ignorance, one does not know what God is, how to become happy, or why we are in this world. For example, if you take an animal to the slaughterhouse, it will go. This is ignorance. But a man will protest. If a goat is to be killed in five minutes, it will be happy because it is eating a morsel of grass. Just like even if you are planning to kill a child, he is happy and laughs because he is innocent. That is ignorance.

Bob: Being in these modes determines your *karma*. Is that correct?

Śrīla Prabhupāda: Yes. According to the association of the modes of nature, your activities are being contaminated. *Kāraṇaṁ guṇa-saṅgo 'sya sad-asad-yoni-janmasu:* "A man gets a higher birth or lower birth according to the association of the *guṇas,* or the modes of nature."

Bob: What mode is cheating?

Śrīla Prabhupāda: Cheating is passion mixed with ignorance. Suppose one man cheats another. That means he wants to obtain something; he is passionate. But if he commits murder, he does not know that he will have to suffer for it, so it is ignorance mixed with passion.

Bob: And what about somebody helping another person?

Śrīla Prabhupāda: That is goodness.

Bob: Why is that goodness? You said that goodness is when you have knowledge. What intelligence is that? It represents knowledge of what?

Śrīla Prabhupāda: Helping another person means that he is ignorant and you are trying to enlighten him.

Bob: So giving intelligence is goodness?

Śrīla Prabhupāda: Yes.

Bob: And what about just giving assistance?

Śrīla Prabhupāda: That is also goodness.

Bob: If a beggar has nothing and you give him alms, what is that?

Śrīla Prabhupāda: That may still be goodness. But in your Bowery Street, they give some charity to a man and he immediately purchases a bottle of wine, which he drinks and then passes out. So that is charity. But that is not goodness; that is ignorance.

Bob: Charity is ignorance?

Śrīla Prabhupāda: There are three kinds of charities — good, passionate and ignorant. Goodness is giving charity where charity must be given. Just like this Kṛṣṇa consciousness movement, if anyone gives charity to this movement, that is goodness because it is spreading God consciousness, Kṛṣṇa consciousness. That is goodness. If one gives charity for some return, that is passion. And if someone gives charity in an improper place and time, without respect and to a person who may misuse the gift, that is ignorance. But Kṛṣṇa says, *yat karoṣi yad aśnāsi yaj juhoṣi dadāsi yat:* "All that you do, all that you eat, all that you offer and give away, as well as all austerities that you may perform, should be done as an offering unto Me." If Kṛṣṇa takes what you offer, that is the perfection of charity. Or anyone who is a representative of Kṛṣṇa — if he takes, that is perfection.

Bob: And what kind of charity is it when you give food to someone who is hungry?

Śrīla Prabhupāda: Well, that depends on the circumstances. For example, if a doctor forbids his patient to take any solid food, and if the patient asks, "Give me some solids," and if you give him solid food in charity, then you are not doing good to him. Your action is ignorance.

Bob: Are devotees beyond accumulating *karma?* These devotees, do they feel *karma?* Do they work in these modes? Are they in the mode of goodness?

Śrīla Prabhupāda: They are above goodness — *śuddha-sattva.* Devotees are not in this material world; they are in the spiritual world. That is stated in the *Bhagavad-gītā*:

māṁ ca yo 'vyabhicāreṇa
bhakti-yogena sevate
sa guṇān samatītyaitān
brahma-bhūyāya kalpate

["One who engages in full devotional service, unfailing in all circumstances, at once transcends the modes of material nature and thus comes to the level of Brahman."] Devotees are neither in goodness, passion, nor ignorance; they are transcendental to all these qualities.

Bob: A devotee who is very faithful reaches this stage?

Śrīla Prabhupāda: Yes. You can become a devotee as they have become. It is not difficult. Simply you have to engage yourself in the transcendental loving service of the Lord, that's all.

Bob: Śrīla Prabhupāda, what is the status of service minus devotion?

Śrīla Prabhupāda: Hm-m? That is not service, that is business. For example, here in Māyāpur we have employed a contractor. That is not service — that is business. Is it not? Sometimes they will advertise, "Our customers are our masters." Is it not? But in spite of the flowery language — "Our customers are our masters" — this is business, because nobody is a qualified customer unless he pays. But service is not like that. Caitanya Mahāprabhu prays to Kṛṣṇa, *yathā tathā vā vidadhātu lampaṭo mat-prāṇa-nāthas tu sa eva nāparaḥ:* "You do whatever You like, but still You are my worshipable Lord." That is service. "I don't ask any return from You." That is service. When you expect some return, that is business.

Bob: I wish to gain more knowledge of God and be able to feel God's presence more. The reason for this is because I feel life has little meaning without this.

Śrīla Prabhupāda: Yes! If you miss this human form of life, then it is a great loss. That is a great chance given to the living entity to get out of the entanglement of material existence.

Bob: I feel thankful that I've been able to ask these questions.

Śrīla Prabhupāda: Yes, you can learn more and more. Questions and answers are required. They are beneficial to all. Suta Gosvāmī says:

munayaḥ sādhu pṛṣṭo 'haṁ
bhavadbhir loka-maṅgalam
yat kṛtaḥ kṛṣṇa-sampraśno
yenātmā suprasīdati

["O sages, I have been justly questioned by you. Your questions are worthy because they relate to Lord Kṛṣṇa and so are relevant to the world's welfare. Only questions of this sort are capable of completely satisfying the self."] *Kṛṣṇa-sampraśnah.* That is very good. When you discuss and hear, that is *loka-maṅgalam,* auspicious for everyone. Both the questions and the answers.

Bob: But I still have my connections at home. I am engaged.

Śrīla Prabhupāda: No, no, that's not a problem. He is married. [*He indicates Śyāmasundara.*] Marriage is no barrier. There are four different orders of spiritual life: *brahmacārī, gṛhastha, vānaprastha* and *sannyāsa.* So after *brahmacārī* life, one can marry, but it is not obligatory. One may remain *naiṣṭika-brahmacārī* — unmarried for his whole life. But a regular *brahmacārī* may marry. And, after marriage, there is *vānaprastha* life. This means that one is a little aloof from family; the husband and wife live separately. At that time there is no sex life. Then when he is fully renounced, detached from family life, he takes *sannyāsa.*

Bob: Does a *sannyāsī* forget his wife completely then?

Śrīla Prabhupāda: Yes. Forgetting is not very difficult, if you try. Out of sight, out of mind. I also have my wife, children, grandchildren; but out of sight, out of mind. That's all. Therefore, *vānaprastha, sannyāsa* — everything is nicely arranged in the Vedic system.

FIVE

Becoming Pure
February 29, 1972

Bob: I met someone who came here today because he heard there were hippies in Māyāpur.
Śrīla Prabhupāda: He's Indian?
Bob: Yes. He told me that when he was young he faithfully worshipped the demigoddess Kālī every day. But then the floods came, and all the people saw was hardship, so he gave up that religion. He says he finds his happiness in trying to develop love among people. He thinks that after he dies he might become part of God, but he doesn't want to worry about it now. He's tried religious experiences, but they haven't worked. I bring this up because in America I come across a lot of people like this. They see that religion, like his worship of Kali or other kinds of religion they've experienced, doesn't work. And I don't know what to say to people like him to convince them it's worth trying to add God and religion to their lives.
Śrīla Prabhupāda: Do not try at the present moment. You try to be convinced yourself. *You* first of all be convinced. And then try to convince others. Caitanya Mahāprabhu's instruction is that you can improve the welfare of others when your own life is a success:

bhārata-bhūmite haila manuṣya-janma yāra
janma sārthaka kari 'kara para-upakāra

First make your life perfect. Then try to teach others.

Bob: The devotees told me that without consciousness of Kṛṣṇa, you cannot be happy. Yet at times I feel happy.

Śrīla Prabhupāda: At times. Not always.

Bob: Yes.

Śrīla Prabhupāda: But if you become Kṛṣṇa conscious, you will feel happy always.

Bob: They implied that without Kṛṣṇa consciousness I cannot feel happy.

Śrīla Prabhupāda: That is a fact. For example, if you are a land animal and you are thrown into water, you cannot be happy. When again you are on land, then you'll be happy. Similarly, we are part and parcel of Kṛṣṇa; we cannot be happy without being part and parcel of Kṛṣṇa. Just without the machine, the part has no value, but when it is put into the machine it has value. We are part of Kṛṣṇa; we must join Kṛṣṇa. And immediately by your consciousness you can join Kṛṣṇa. Simply by thinking, "I am Kṛṣṇa's. Kṛṣṇa is mine." That is our actual position.

Bob: We are part of Kṛṣṇa.

Śrīla Prabhupāda: Yes. Everything is part and parcel of Kṛṣṇa, because everything is generated by the energy of Kṛṣṇa and everything is the energy of Kṛṣṇa.

Bob: How can I come to feel closer to God? At times I come to the temple, and then I leave. But I'm not sure how much I take with me.

Śrīla Prabhupāda: You have to be purified. It does not take much time. Within six months you will realise your progress. But you have to follow the regulative principles; then it will be all right, just as these boys and girls are doing.

They have no tendency to go to the cinema or a club. No. They have stopped all *anarthas,* all unnecessary things. The whole of human life is meant for purification. *Tapo divyaṁ putrakā yena sattvaṁ śuddhyed yasmād brahma-saukhyaṁ tv anantam.*

Sattva means existence. If you don't purify your existence, then you will have to change from this body to that. Sometimes it may be higher, sometimes lower. For example, if you don't cure a disease, it can cause you so much trouble. Similarly, if you don't purify your existence, then you will have to transmigrate from one body to another. These are very subtle laws of nature, and there is no guarantee that you will get a very comfortable body or even an American body. Therefore, it is essential for a human being to purify his existence. Unless you purify your existence you will hanker after happiness but will not always be happy.

Bob: When I go to my job in New York, I hope I'll become pure, but I'm sure that I won't become as pure as your devotees here. I don't see myself doing that.

Śrīla Prabhupāda: You can do as they are doing. They were not pure in the beginning; now they are pure. Similarly, you can become pure. Just like in your childhood you were not educated, but now you are educated. If you are serious, you can keep yourself pure anywhere. It doesn't matter whether you stay in America or India. But you must know how to keep yourself purified. That's all. For instance, I went to America. But either in America or in India, I am the same man.

Bob: I have tried somewhat to follow these principles since I met you the first time.

Śrīla Prabhupāda: But you must *strictly* follow if you are serious.

Bob: Maybe, OK, maybe. What I say now is, well, the most foolish of all I've said.

Śrīla Prabhupāda: No, no, not foolish. I don't say foolish — but imperfect.

Bob: Right now I admire and respect your devotees, but I don't feel as if I am part of them, or even that I have a great desire to be part of them. I feel that I just want to do what is right, come closer to God; and if I just go to a better life next time I'll be satisfied.

Śrīla Prabhupāda: Very good. So, just follow in their footsteps, and your desire will be fulfilled. We are training people how to become purified and happy. That is our mission. We want to see everyone happy. *Sarve sukhino bhavantu.* People do not know how to become happy. They do not take the standard path to become happy. They manufacture their own way; that is the difficulty. Therefore, Ṛṣabhadeva advised his sons: "My dear boys, just undergo austerity for transcendental realisation." Everyone is performing austerity. One boy I know — he had to go to a foreign country to learn commercial management. Now he is well situated. In this way everyone must undergo some austerity for his future life. So why not take that austerity for *permanent* happiness?

You have to purify your existence and your body. As many times as you accept a material body, you will have to change it. But as soon as you get a spiritual body, there is no question of change. Although we already have a spiritual body, due to our present material contamination we are developing a material body. But if we practise spiritual life, then we shall develop a spiritual body. If you put an iron rod within fire, it will become like fire. Is it not?

Bob: Yes.

Śrīla Prabhupāda: Similarly, if you always keep yourself spiritually engaged, your body will act spiritually, although it is material. When an iron rod is red-hot, you can touch it anywhere, and it will burn. It takes on the quality of fire. So, if you always keep yourself in Kṛṣṇa consciousness, then you will become spiritualised. You will act spiritually. No more material demands.

Bob: How do I do this?

Śrīla Prabhupāda: This process. You have seen these six boys who have been initiated today. They are doing it; it is very simple. You have to follow the four restrictive regulations and chant on these beads. Very easy.

Bob: Well, but, I follow some of these regulative principles now, but not all.

Śrīla Prabhupāda: "Some" means? There are only four regulative principles. So "some" means three, or two?

Bob: I follow one or two.

Śrīla Prabhupāda: Why not the other three? What is the difficulty? Which one do you follow?

Bob: Well, I'm almost vegetarian, but I eat eggs.

Śrīla Prabhupāda: Then that is also not complete.

Bob: I've become vegetarian since time November, but . . .

Śrīla Prabhupāda: Vegetarian is no qualification. The pigeon is vegetarian. The monkey, the most rubbish creature, is vegetarian and he lives naked in the forest — and is the most mischievous.

Bob: I felt that it was a little bit of progress. It was somewhat difficult at first, then easy.

Śrīla Prabhupāda: You can stick to all the regulative principles, provided you take to the Kṛṣṇa consciousness process. Otherwise it is not possible.

Bob: Yes, this is it. Sometimes when I'm back in Bihar with my friends, and there's nothing to do but fight mosquitoes in the evening, they say, "How about smoking some marijuana?" I agree, "Sure, there's nothing else to do." Then I sit down and enjoy myself for the evening. We were doing this every day, and eventually we realised we were hurting ourselves, so we stopped. But still on occasion we . . .

Śrīla Prabhupāda: You have to live with *us*. Then your friends will not ask you, "What about marijuana?" Keep the association of devotees. We are opening centres to give people a chance to associate with us. That's why we have taken so much land in Māyāpur. Those who are seriously desirous — they will come and live with us. Association is very influential. If you associate with drunkards, you become a drunk; if you associate with *sādhus,* then you become a *sādhu.*

Śyāmasundara: He can come and stay with you in Bombay.

Śrīla Prabhupāda: Yes, you can stay with us in Bombay. But you want friends with marijuana. That is the difficulty.

Bob: Let me ask you about something else; then maybe I'll come back to this. I find that I think of myself too much, and this way I can't think of God so much. I think of myself in too many places. How can I forget about myself so I can concentrate on other, more important things?

Śrīla Prabhupāda: As these devotees have done.

Bob: You are saying to me that my path — I think that you're saying my path to purity is to become a devotee.

Śrīla Prabhupāda: Do you hesitate?

Bob: Well, I . . .

Śrīla Prabhupāda: Is it very difficult to become a devotee?

Bob: For myself it is. I don't feel so much the desire. First the devotees tell me that they have given up material life. These four regulative principles, they have explained to me, mean giving up material life, and that I see.

Śrīla Prabhupāda: What do you mean by material life? I am sitting on this bed. Is it material or spiritual?

Bob: Material.

Śrīla Prabhupāda: Then how have we given up material life?

Bob: I think how I interpreted it was "a desire for our material gains".

Śrīla Prabhupāda: What is material?

Bob: Working towards material gains and not giving up all materials.
Śrīla Prabhupāda: Material life means when you desire to gratify your senses; that is material life. And when you desire to serve God, that is spiritual life. That is the difference between material life and spiritual life. Now we are trying to serve our senses. But instead of serving the senses, we serve God — that is spiritual life. What is the difference between our activities and others' activities? We are using everything — table, chair, bed, tape recorder, typewriter — so what is the difference? The difference is that we are using everything for Kṛṣṇa.
Bob: The devotees have said that the sensual pleasures they have given up are replaced with spiritual pleasures. But I haven't felt this in my own life.
Śrīla Prabhupāda: Spiritual pleasures come when you desire to please Kṛṣṇa. That is spiritual pleasure. For example, a mother is more pleased by feeding her son. She's not eating, but when she sees that her son is eating very nicely, then she becomes pleased.
Bob: Spiritual pleasure, then, is pleasing God.
Śrīla Prabhupāda: Yes. Spiritual pleasure means the pleasure of Kṛṣṇa. Material pleasure means the pleasure of the senses. That's all. This is the difference. When you simply try to please Kṛṣṇa, that is spiritual pleasure.
Bob: My thought of pleasing God was to —
Śrīla Prabhupāda: Don't manufacture your ways of pleasing God. Suppose I want to please you. Then I shall ask you, "How can I serve you?" Not that I manufacture some service; that is not pleasing. Suppose I want a glass of water. If you concoct the idea, "Swamiji will be more pleased if I give him a glass of hot milk," that will not please me. If you want to please me, then you should ask me, "How can

I please you?" And if you do what I order, that will please me.

Bob: And pleasing Kṛṣṇa, then, is being a devotee of Kṛṣṇa?

Śrīla Prabhupāda: A devotee is one who is always pleasing Kṛṣṇa. He has no other business. That is a devotee.

Bob: Can you tell me some more about chanting Hare Kṛṣṇa? I have chanted for quite some time, but never regularly — just a little bit here and there. I just got beads very recently, and once in a while I feel comfortable chanting, but once in a while not comfortable at all. Maybe I don't chant properly. I don't know.

Śrīla Prabhupāda: Yes, everything has a process. You have to adopt the process.

Bob: The devotees tell me of the ecstasy they feel when chanting.

Śrīla Prabhupāda: Yes, the more you become purified, the more you will feel ecstasy. This chanting is the purifying process.

SIX

Spiritual Discipline
February 29, 1972, evening

Bob: Śrīla Prabhupāda, if we don't practise austerities voluntarily, then must we involuntarily practise some austerities?
Śrīla Prabhupāda: Yes, under the direction of the spiritual master. You have no mind to follow austerities, but when you accept a spiritual master, you have to carry out his order. That is austerity.
Śyāmasundara: Even if you don't want to practise austerity, you must?
Śrīla Prabhupāda: Yes, you must. Because you have surrendered to your spiritual master, his order is final. So even if you don't like it, you have to do it. To please me. But you don't like. Nobody likes to fast, but the spiritual master says, "Today, fasting." So what can be done? A disciple is one who has voluntarily agreed to be disciplined by the spiritual master. That is austerity.
Śyāmasundara: Many people in the material world who may be completely enamoured by material life don't want to undergo austerity or bodily pain, but still they must. They are being forced by nature to suffer austerities. Is that right?
Śrīla Prabhupāda: That is forced austerity. That is not good. Only voluntary austerity will help.
Śyāmasundara: If you don't undergo voluntary austerity, then are you forced to undergo austerity?
Śrīla Prabhupāda: That is the difference between man and

animal. An animal cannot accept austerity, but a man can accept it. When a man sees some nice food in the confectioner's shop, he may want to eat it. But seeing that he has no money, he can restrain himself. But when a cow comes, she immediately pushes her mouth in. You can even beat her with a stick, but she will tolerate it. Therefore, an animal cannot undergo austerity.

Our austerity, however, is very nice. We chant Hare Kṛṣṇa, dance, and then Kṛṣṇa sends very nice food, and we eat. That's all. Why are you not agreeable to such austerity? Chanting, dancing and eating nicely? Because we are following austerities, Kṛṣṇa sends us nice things. So we are not losers. When you become Kṛṣṇa-ised, then you get *more* comforts than at the present moment. That's a fact. I have been living alone for the last twenty years, but I have no difficulties. Before taking *sannyāsa* I was living in Delhi. And although I was living alone, I had no difficulties.

Śyāmasundara: If you don't accept spiritual discipline, does nature force calamities?

Śrīla Prabhupāda: Oh, yes. That is stated in the *Bhagavad-gītā*:

daivī hy eṣā guṇamayī
mama māyā duratyayā
mām eva ye prapadyante
māyām etāṁ taranti te

["This divine energy of Mine, consisting of the three modes of material nature, is difficult to overcome. But those who have surrendered unto Me can easily cross beyond it."] *Māyā* is imposing so many difficulties, but as soon as you surrender to Kṛṣṇa, no more imposition.

Śyāmasundara: We are so foolish that we are always thinking, "In the future I'll be happy."

Śrīla Prabhupāda: Yes, that is *māyā,* illusion. That is like the ass. You sit down on the back of the ass and hold a morsel of grass before its face. The ass is thinking, "Let me go forward a little, and I shall get the grass." But it is always one foot distant. That is ass-ism. Everyone is thinking, "Let me go a little forward, and I'll get it. I'll be very happy."

[*There is a long pause, filled with the sound of bicycle horns, children playing, and throngs of people calling one another.*]

Bob: I thank you so much. Tomorrow I'll have to leave you.

Śrīla Prabhupāda: Don't talk l-e-a-v-e, but talk l-i-v-e.

Bob: I cannot yet. I must return to my town tomorrow.

Śrīla Prabhupāda: Don't return.

Bob: I should stay here tomorrow?

Śrīla Prabhupāda: Stay here.

Bob: If you tell me to, I'll stay.

Śrīla Prabhupāda: Yes, you are a very good boy.

[*Chanting starts somewhere in the background, with exotic* mṛdaṅga *drumbeats amidst laughing and the loud blowing of horns.*]

Śrīla Prabhupāda: It is very simple. When the living entities forget Kṛṣṇa, they are in this material world. Kṛṣṇa means His name, His form, His abode, His pastimes — everything. When we speak of a king, it means the king's government, king's palace, king's queen, king's sons, secretaries, military strength — everything. Is it not?

Bob: Yes.

Śrīla Prabhupāda: Similarly, Kṛṣṇa is the Supreme Personality of Godhead, so as soon as we think of Kṛṣṇa, this means all the energies of Kṛṣṇa. That is complete by saying, "Rādhā-Kṛṣṇa". Rādhā represents all the energy of Kṛṣṇa. And Kṛṣṇa is the Supreme Lord. So when we speak of Kṛṣṇa, the living entities are also included because the living entities are energies, different energies of Kṛṣṇa — superior energy. So when this energy is not serving the energetic, that is material existence. The whole world is serving

Kṛṣṇa in a different way. They are serving indirectly, just as disobedient citizens serve the government indirectly. Prisoners come to the prison house on account of their disobedience of the laws of the state. So, in the prison house, they are forced to obey the laws of the state. Similarly, all the living entities here are godless, either by ignorance or by choice. They do not like to accept the supremacy of God. Demoniac. So we are trying to bring them to their original condition. That is the Kṛṣṇa consciousness movement.

Bob: I'd like to ask you something I talked with devotees about: medicine. I walked to the river with some devotees today. I have a cold, so I said I shouldn't go in the water. Some felt I should because it is the Ganges, and some said I shouldn't because I have a cold; and we were talking, and I don't understand. Do we get sick because of our bad actions in the past?

Śrīla Prabhupāda: Yes, that's a fact. Any kind of distress we suffer is due to our impious activities in the past.

Bob: But when someone is removed from karmic influence does he still get sick?

Śrīla Prabhupāda: Even if he gets sick, that is temporary. For instance, this fan is moving. If you disconnect the electric power, then the fan will move for a moment. That movement is not due to the electric current. That is force, momentum. But as soon as it stops, no more movement. Similarly, if a devotee who has surrendered to Kṛṣṇa is suffering from material consequences, that is temporary. Therefore, a devotee does not take any material miseries as miseries. He takes them as Kṛṣṇa's, God's, mercy.

Bob: Is that true only for a perfected soul, a pure devotee?

Śrīla Prabhupāda: A perfected soul is one who engages twenty-four hours a day in Kṛṣṇa consciousness. That is perfection. That is a transcendental position. Perfection means to engage in one's original consciousness. That is stated in

Bhagavad-gītā, sve sve karmaṇy abhirataḥ saṁsiddhiṁ labhate naraḥ: "By following his qualities of work, every man can become perfect." Complete perfection. *Saṁsiddhi. Sam* means complete. *Siddhi* is perfection. That is Brahman realisation, spiritual realisation. And *saṁsiddhi* means devotion, which comes after Brahman realisation.

In the *Bhagavad-gītā* it is stated that one who goes back home, back to Godhead, has attained the complete perfection. So perfection comes when one realises that he is not this body; he is spirit soul. *Brahma-bhūta* — that is called Brahman realisation. That is perfection. And *saṁsiddhi* comes after Brahman realisation, when one engages in devotional service. Therefore if one is already engaged in devotional service, it is to be understood that Brahman realisation is there. Therefore it is called *saṁsiddhi.*

Bob: I ask you this very humbly, but do you personally feel diseases and sickness?

Śrīla Prabhupāda: Yes.

Bob: Is this a result of your past *karma?*

Śrīla Prabhupāda: Yes.

Bob: So one in this material world never escapes his *karma* completely? Even a pure devotee?

Śrīla Prabhupāda: Yes, he escapes. No more *karma* for a devotee. No more karmic reaction.

Bob: But you must be the best devotee.

Śrīla Prabhupāda: No, I don't consider myself the best devotee. I am the lowest. *You* are the best devotee.

Bob: Oh, no, no! What you say always seems right. So, then you must be the best devotee.

Śrīla Prabhupāda: The thing is that even the best devotee comes to the platform of a second-class devotee when he preaches.

Bob: What would the best devotee be doing?

Śrīla Prabhupāda: The best devotee does not preach.
Bob: What does he do?
Śrīla Prabhupāda: He sees there is no need of preaching. For him, everyone is a devotee. He sees no more nondevotees — all devotees. He is called an *uttama-adhikārī.* But while I am preaching, how can I say I am the best devotee? Just like Rādhārāṇī, Kṛṣṇa's consort. She does not see anyone as a nondevotee. Therefore we try to approach Radharani. If anyone approaches Rādhārāṇī, She recommends to Kṛṣṇa, "Here is the best devotee. He is better than Me," and Kṛṣṇa cannot refuse to accept him. That is the best devotee. But that is not to be imitated. One should never think, "I have become the best devotee."

īśvare tad-adhīneṣu
bāliśeṣu dviṣatsu ca
prema-maitrī-kṛpopekṣā
yaḥ karoti sa madhyamah

A second-class devotee has the vision that some are envious of God, but this is not the vision of the best devotee. The best devotee sees, "Nobody is envious of God. Everyone is better than me." Just like *Caitanya-caritāmṛta's* author, Kṛṣṇadāsa Kavirāja, says, "I am lower than the worm in the stool." *Purīṣera kīṭa haite muñi se laghiṣṭha.* He is not making a show. He is feeling like that. "I am the lowest. Everyone is best, but I am the lowest. Everyone is engaged in Kṛṣṇa's service. I am not engaged." Caitanya Mahāprabhu said, "Oh, I have not a pinch of devotion to Kṛṣṇa. I make a show of crying. If I had been a devotee of Kṛṣṇa, I would have died long ago. But I am living. That is the proof that I do not love Kṛṣṇa." That is the vision of the best devotee. He is so much absorbed in Kṛṣṇa's love that he says,

"Everything is going on, but I am the lowest. Therefore I cannot see God." That is the best devotee.

Bob: So a devotee must work for everybody's liberation?

Śrīla Prabhupāda: Yes. A devotee must work under the direction of a bona fide spiritual master, not imitate the best devotee.

Śyāmasundara: One time you said that sometimes you feel sickness or pain due to the sinful activities of your devotees. Can disease sometimes be due to that?

Śrīla Prabhupāda: You see, Kṛṣṇa says, *ahaṁ tvāṁ sarva-pāpebhyo mokṣayiṣyāmi mā śucaḥ:* "I will deliver you from all sinful reaction. Do not fear." So Kṛṣṇa is so powerful that He can immediately take up all the sins of others and immediately make them right. But when a living entity plays the part on behalf of Kṛṣṇa, he also takes the responsibility for the sinful activities of his devotees. Therefore to become a guru is not an easy task. You see? He has to take all the poisons and absorb them. So because he is not Kṛṣṇa, sometimes there is some trouble. Therefore Caitanya Mahāprabhu has forbidden, "Don't make many *śiṣyas,* many disciples." But for preaching work we have to accept many disciples, for expanding preaching — even if we suffer. That's a fact. The spiritual master has to take the responsibility for all the sinful activities of his disciples. Therefore to make many disciples is a risky job unless one is able to assimilate all the sins.

vāñchā-kalpa-tarubhyaś ca
kṛpā-sindhubhya eva ca
patitānāṁ pāvanebhyo
vaiṣṇavebhyo namo namaḥ

["I offer my respectful obeisances unto all the Vaiṣṇava devotees of the Lord. They are just like desire trees who can fulfil the desires of everyone, and they are full of compassion for the fallen conditioned souls."] He takes responsibility for all the fallen souls. That idea is also in the Bible. Jesus Christ took all the sinful reactions of the people and sacrificed his life. That is the responsibility of a spiritual master. Because Kṛṣṇa is Kṛṣṇa, He is *apāpa-viddha* — He cannot be attacked by sinful reactions. But a living entity is sometimes subjected to their influence because he is so small. Like a big fire and a small fire. If you put some big thing in a small fire, the fire itself may be extinguished. But in a big fire, whatever you put in is all right. The big fire can consume anything.

Bob: Christ's suffering was of that nature?

Śrīla Prabhupāda: He took the sinful reactions of all the people; therefore he suffered. He said that he took all the sinful reactions of the people and sacrificed his life. But Christians have made it a law that Christ should suffer while they do all nonsense. They are such great fools! They have let Jesus Christ make a contract to take all their sinful reactions so they can go on with all nonsense. That is how they take their religion. Christ was so magnanimous that he took all their sins and suffered, but that hasn't induced them to *stop* all these sins. They have not yet come to that sense. They have taken it very easily: "Let Lord Jesus Christ suffer, and we'll do all nonsense." Is it not?

Bob: It is so.

Śrīla Prabhupāda: They should be ashamed: "Lord Jesus Christ suffered for us, yet we are continuing with our sinful activities." He told everyone, "Thou shalt not kill," but they are indulging in killing, thinking, "Lord Jesus Christ will excuse us and take all the sinful reactions." This is going on.

We should be very cautious: "For my sinful actions my spiritual master will suffer, so I'll not commit even a pinch of sinful activities." That is the duty of the disciple. After initiation, all sinful reaction is finished. Now if he again commits sinful activities, his spiritual master has to suffer. A disciple should be sympathetic and consider that for his sinful activities, his spiritual master will suffer. If the spiritual master is attacked by some disease, it is due to the sinful activities of others. "Don't make many disciples." But we do it because we are preaching. Never mind, let us suffer; still we shall accept these disciples.

Now your question was when I suffer is it due to my past misdeeds? Was it not? *That is my misdeed* — that I accepted some disciples who are nonsense. That is my misdeed.

Bob: This happens on occasions?

Śrīla Prabhupāda: Yes. This is sure to happen because we are accepting so many men. It is the duty of the disciples to be cautious and think, "My spiritual master has saved me. I should not put him into suffering again." When the spiritual master suffers, Kṛṣṇa saves him. Kṛṣṇa thinks, "Oh, he has taken so much responsibility for delivering a fallen person." So Kṛṣṇa is there: *kaunteya pratijānīhi na me bhaktaḥ praṇaśyati.* ["O son of Kunti, declare it boldly that My devotee never perishes."] This is because the spiritual master takes the risk on account of Kṛṣṇa.

Bob: Your suffering is not the same kind of pain.

Śrīla Prabhupāda: No, it is not due to *karma.* The pain is there sometimes, so that the disciples may know, "Due to our sinful activities, our spiritual master is suffering."

Bob: You look very well now.

Śrīla Prabhupāda: I am always well in the sense that even if there is suffering, I know Kṛṣṇa will protect me. But this suffering is not due to *my* sinful activities.

Bob: I drink boiled water because some of the water has disease in it. But why should I have to drink boiled water if I have been good enough not to get a disease? I should be able to drink any water. And if I have been not acting properly, then I'll get disease anyway.

Śrīla Prabhupāda: As long as you are in the material world, you cannot neglect physical laws. Suppose you go to a jungle and there is a tiger. It is known that it will attack you, so why should you voluntarily go and be attacked? It is not that a devotee should take physical risks while he has a physical body. It is not that now that I have become a devotee, I challenge everything. That is foolishness.

anāsaktasya viṣayān
yathārham upayuñjataḥ
nirbandhaḥ kṛṣṇa-sambandhe
yuktaṁ vairāgyam ucyate

A devotee is advised to accept the necessities of life without attachment. He'll take boiled water. But if boiled water is not available, does it mean he will not drink water? If it is not available, he will drink ordinary water. We take Kṛṣṇa *prasādam,* but while touring, sometimes we have to take some food in a hotel. Because one is a devotee, should he think, "I will not take any food from the hotel. I shall starve"? If I starve, then I will be weak and will not be able to preach.

Bob: Does a devotee lose some of his individuality?

Śrīla Prabhupāda: No, he has full individuality for pleasing Kṛṣṇa. Kṛṣṇa says, "You surrender unto Me." So the devotee voluntarily surrenders. It is not that he has lost his individuality. He keeps his individuality. Just like in the beginning Arjuna declined to fight, on account of his individuality. But when he accepted Kṛṣṇa as his spiritual master, he became *śiṣya,* a disciple. Then whatever Kṛṣṇa ordered, he said yes. That doesn't mean he lost his individuality. He voluntarily accepted: "Whatever Kṛṣṇa says, I shall do." Just like all my disciples — they have not lost their individuality, but they have surrendered their individuality. That is required. For example, suppose a man does not use sex. It does not mean he has become impotent. If he likes, he can have sex a thousand times. But he has voluntarily avoided it. *Paraṁ dṛṣṭvā nivartate:* He has a higher taste. Sometimes we fast, but that does not mean we are diseased. We voluntarily fast. It does not mean that I am not hungry or cannot eat. But we voluntarily fast.

Bob: Does the devotee who surrenders keep his individual taste for different things? Does he keep his individual likes and dislikes?

Śrīla Prabhupāda: Yes, he keeps everything in full. But he gives preference to Kṛṣṇa. Suppose I like this thing but Kṛṣṇa says, "No, you cannot use it." Then I shall not use it. That is for Kṛṣṇa's sake. Kṛṣṇa says positively, "I like these things." So we have to offer to Kṛṣṇa what He likes, and then we'll take *prasādam.* Kṛṣṇa likes Rādhārāṇī. Therefore all the *gopīs* are trying to push Rādhārāṇī to Kṛṣṇa. They think, "Kṛṣṇa likes this *gopī.* All right, push Her forward to Him." That is Kṛṣṇa consciousness. To satisfy the senses of Kṛṣṇa, not to satisfy my senses. That is *bhakti.* That is called *prema,* love for Kṛṣṇa. "Ah, Kṛṣṇa likes this. I must give Him this."

Bob: I like some of the *prasādam* offered to Kṛṣṇa, but some is not at all to my liking.

Śrīla Prabhupāda: You should not do that. The perfection is that you should accept whatever is offered to Kṛṣṇa. That is perfection. You cannot say, "I like this, I don't like this." So long as you make such discrimination, that means you have not appreciated what *prasādam* is. No disliking, no liking. Whatever Kṛṣṇa likes, that's all right.

Bob: But what if someone prepares some *prasādam* for Kṛṣṇa but he does not make it nicely?

Śrīla Prabhupāda: No, if made sincerely with devotion, then Kṛṣṇa will like it. Vidura was feeding Kṛṣṇa bananas, but he was so absorbed in thoughts of Kṛṣṇa that he was throwing away the real bananas and giving Kṛṣṇa the skins. And Kṛṣṇa was eating. Kṛṣṇa knew that Vidura was giving Him the skins in devotion. Kṛṣṇa can eat anything, provided there is devotion; it doesn't matter whether it is materially tasteful or not. Similarly, a devotee also takes Kṛṣṇa *prasādam*, whether it is tasty or not. We should accept everything.
Bob: But what if the devotion is not there?
Śrīla Prabhupāda: If devotion is not present, Kṛṣṇa doesn't like any food, whether it's tasty or not. He does not accept it.
Bob: In India somebody may cook these types of foods . . .
Śrīla Prabhupāda: Oh, India, India. Don't talk of India! Talk of philosophy. If there is not devotion, Kṛṣṇa does not accept anything, either in India or in your country. Lord Kṛṣṇa is not obliged to accept anything just because it is very tasty or costly. Kṛṣṇa has very many delicious dishes in Vaikuṇṭha; He is not hankering after your food. He accepts your devotion, *bhakti.* The real thing is devotion, not the food. Kṛṣṇa does not accept any food of this material world. He accepts only the devotion.

patraṁ puṣpaṁ phalaṁ toyaṁ
yo me bhaktyā prayacchati
ahaṁ bhakty-upahṛtam
aśnāmi prayatātmanaḥ

"If one offers Me with love and devotion a leaf, a flower, fruit or water, I will accept it, because it has been offered to Me with devotion and love." That is required. Therefore we do not allow anyone to cook who is not a devotee. Kṛṣṇa does not accept anything from the hands of a non-devotee. Why should He accept? He is not hungry. He does not require any food. He accepts only the devotion, that's all. That is the main point. So one has to become a devotee, not a good cook. But if he is a devotee, then he will be a good cook also. Automatically he will become a good cook. Therefore one has to become a devotee only; then all other good qualifications will automatically be there. And if he is a nondevotee, any good qualifications he possesses have no value. He is on the mental plane, so he has no good qualification.

Bob: I still do not understand so much about *prasādam.*

Śrīla Prabhupāda: *Prasādam* is always *prasādam.* But because we are not elevated sufficiently, we do not like some *prasādam.*

Bob: I found that some *prasādam* is too spicy and hurts my stomach.

Śrīla Prabhupāda: Well, that is also due to not appreciating, but the cook should have consideration. Kṛṣṇa must be offered first-class foodstuffs. So if the cook offers something last-class, he is not performing his duty. But Kṛṣṇa can accept anything if it is offered by a devotee, and a devotee can accept any *prasādam,* even if it is spicy. Hiranyakasipu gave his son poison, and after offering it to Kṛṣṇa, the son drank it as nectar. So even if it is spicy to others' taste, it is very palatable to the devotee. What is the question of spicy? Kṛṣṇa was offered poison, real poison. Pūtanā Rākṣasī offered baby Kṛṣṇa poison on her breast for Him to suck. But Kṛṣṇa is so nice that He thought, "She came to Me as My mother," so He took the poison and delivered her. Kṛṣṇa does not take the bad side. A good man does not take the bad side; he takes only the good side. Just like one of my Godbrothers. He had the motivation to do business with my Guru Mahārāja [spiritual master], but my Guru Mahārāja did not take the bad side. He took the good side. He thought, "He has come forward to give me some service."

Bob: Devotees sometimes have some trouble, and so do not eat a certain type of food — like some ghee because of liver trouble. Should these devotees take all kinds of *prasādam*?

Śrīla Prabhupāda: No, no. Those who are not perfect devotees may discriminate. But a perfect devotee does not discriminate. Why should you imitate a perfect devotee? So long as you have discrimination, you are not a perfect devotee. So why should you artificially imitate a perfect devotee and eat everything?

The point is, a perfect devotee does not make any discrimination. Whatever is offered to Kṛṣṇa is nectar. That's all. Kṛṣṇa accepts anything from a devotee. Whatever is offered by His devotee He accepts. The same thing is true of a pure devotee. Don't you see the point? A perfect devotee does not make any discrimination. But if I am not a perfect devotee and I discriminate, why shall I imitate the perfect devotee? It may not be possible for me to digest everything because I am not a perfect devotee. A devotee should not be foolish: *kṛṣṇa ye bhaje se baḍa catura.* So a devotee knows his position, and he is intelligent enough to deal with others accordingly.

SEVEN

Acting in Knowledge of Kṛṣṇa February 29, 1972 (evening, continued)

Bob: By what kind of actions does one earn good *karma*?
Śrīla Prabhupāda: Good *karma* means what is prescribed in the *Vedas*. Specifically, it is prescribed that one should perform *yajña*. *Yajña* means actions for the satisfaction of Lord Viṣṇu, the Supreme Personality of Godhead. So good *karma* means performance of the *yajñas* as they are prescribed in the Vedic literatures. And the purpose of this *yajña* is to satisfy the Supreme Lord. A good, law-abiding citizen is one whose actions satisfy the government. So, good *karma* is to satisfy Lord Viṣṇu, the Supreme Lord. Unfortunately, modern civilisation does not know what the Supreme Personality of Godhead is, what to speak of satisfying Him. People do not know. They are simply busy with material activities. Therefore all of them are performing only bad *karma* and therefore suffering. They are blind men leading other blind men. And both are then suffering by bad *karma*. That is very easy to understand. If you do something criminal, you will suffer. If you do something benevolent for the state, for the people, then you are recognised; you are sometimes even given a title. This is good and bad *karma*. So, good *karma* means you enjoy some material

happiness; bad *karma* means you suffer from material distress. By good *karma* you get birth in a good family; you get riches, good money; you become a learned scholar; you become beautiful.

Bob: What about a person who is not very aware of God?

Śrīla Prabhupāda: Then he is an animal. The animal does not know what is good. A person who does not know what is God, or one who does not try to understand what is God, is an animal. Animals have four legs, but that animal has two legs. According to Darwin's theory they are monkeys. So anyone who does not know God, or who does not try to understand God, is nothing but an animal.

Bob: What about innocent people?

Śrīla Prabhupāda: The animal is very innocent. If you cut its throat, it won't protest. The animals are all innocent. Therefore you get the chance to cut their throats. So to become innocent is not a very good qualification. Our proposition is that one must be very, very intelligent, and then he can understand Kṛṣṇa. To become an innocent, ignorant simpleton is not a very good qualification. Simplicity is all right, but one should not be unintelligent.

Bob: Can you tell me what intelligence is?

Śrīla Prabhupāda: Intelligence means to know what one is, what this world is, what God is and their interrelations. The animal does not know what he is. He thinks that he is the body. Similarly, anyone who does not know what he is, is not intelligent.

Bob: What about a person who tries to do what is right and is very conscientious about the things he does? Like the servant who is very honest to his master but knows that if he were not honest he would not be caught. If a person like that stays honest anyway, is that some kind of good *karma*?

Śrīla Prabhupāda: Yes, to become honest is also good *karma*.

How to become a good man is described very elaborately in the *Bhagavad-gītā: daivī sampad vimokṣāya nibandhāyāsurī matā.* So if you become qualified with the *daivī sampad,* transcendental qualities, then *vimokṣāya* — you will be liberated. And, *nibandhāyāsurī* — if you are qualified with the demoniac qualifications, then you will be more and more entangled. Unfortunately modern civilisation does not know what is liberation and what is entanglement. They are so ignorant, they do not know.

If I ask what you mean by liberation, can you answer? And if I ask you what you mean by entanglement, can you answer? These words are there in the Vedic literature: liberation and entanglement. But at the present moment people do not even know what is liberation and what is entanglement. They are so ignorant and foolish, and still they are proud of their advancement in knowledge. You are a professor, a teacher, but can you explain what is liberation?

Bob: Not adequately, because if I could explain, then I would become liberated very soon.

Śrīla Prabhupāda: But if you do not know what is liberation, then there is no question of liberation. It will be neither fast nor slow. You should first know what liberation is. If you do not know where the train is going, then what is the use of understanding whether it is going fast or slow? You do not know your destination so I am asking. You daily ask me. Now I am asking you. What is liberation?

Bob: Ah, okay. I'll need to think for a moment.

Śrīla Prabhupāda: Liberation is described in the *Śrīmad-Bhāgavatam.* The exact Sanskrit word for liberation is *mukti.* So that is defined in the *Śrīmad-Bhāgavatam: muktir hitvānyathā rūpaṁ svarūpeṇa vyavasthitiḥ.* ["Liberation is the permanent situation of the form of the living entity after he gives up the changeable gross and subtle material bodies."] One should stop doing all nonsense, and he must be situated in his original position. But this is even more embarrassing because nobody knows his original position or how to act properly. People are generally acting differently because they do not know what is proper. The modern population is so ignorant about their life. They are in a very awkward position. They do not know.

Bob: Can you tell me who is honest?

Śrīla Prabhupāda: If one does not know what is honesty, how can he be honest? But if you know what is honesty, then you can be honest. First of all you explain what is honesty.

Bob: Honesty is doing what you really feel is right.

Śrīla Prabhupāda: A thief is feeling, "I must steal to provide for my children. It is right." Does it mean that he is honest? The butcher thinks, "It is my life. I must cut the throat of the animals daily." Just like the hunter Mṛgāri. Nārada asked him, "Why are you killing in this way?" And he said, "Oh, it is my business. My father taught it." So he was honestly doing that. A feeling of honesty depends on culture. A thief's culture is different, so he thinks stealing is honest.

Bob: So what is honesty?

Śrīla Prabhupāda: Yes, that is my question. Real honesty is that you should not encroach upon another's property. This is honesty. For instance, this is my table. If you want to take it away while going, is that honesty? So therefore the simple definition of honesty is that you should not encroach upon another's rights. That is honesty.

Bob: So somebody who is honest would be in the mode of goodness? Would that be correct?

Śrīla Prabhupāda: Certainly, certainly. Because the mode of goodness means knowledge. So if you know, "This table does not belong to me; it belongs to Swamiji," you will not try to take it away. Therefore, one must know; then he can be honest.

Bob: You have said that the mode of goodness is knowledge

of God. But somebody may be honest without having very much knowledge of God. Without thinking he is honest because it is God's wishes, someone may just feel like he ought to be honest.
Śrīla Prabhupāda: God wishes everyone to be honest. Why should God think otherwise?
Bob: Can you follow God's wishes without knowing you are following God's wishes?
Śrīla Prabhupāda: No. Following without knowing is absurd. You must know the order of God. And if you follow that, then that is honesty.
Bob: So somebody could not be honest without knowing God?
Śrīla Prabhupāda: Yes, because God is the supreme proprietor, the supreme enjoyer, and He is the supreme friend. That is the statement of the *Bhagavad-gītā.* If anyone knows these three things, then he is in full knowledge. These three things only: that God is the proprietor of everything, God is the friend of everyone, and God is the enjoyer of everything. For example, everyone knows that in the body, the stomach is the enjoyer. Not the hands, legs, eyes, ears. These are there simply to help the stomach. For example the eyes — the vulture goes seven miles up to see where there is food for the stomach. Is it not?
Bob: That is so.
Śrīla Prabhupāda: Then the wings fly there, and the jaws catch the food. Just, as in this body the stomach is the enjoyer, so the central figure of the whole cosmic manifestation, material or spiritual, is Kṛṣṇa, God. He is the enjoyer. We can understand this just by considering our own bodies. The body is also a creation; it has the same mechanical nature you will find in the universe. The same mechanical arrangement will be found anywhere you go, even in animals. The human body or the cosmic manifestation is almost the same

mechanism. So you can understand very easily that in this body — any body, your body — the stomach is the enjoyer. There is a central enjoyer. And the stomach is the friend also. Because if you cannot digest food, all other limbs of the body become weak. Therefore the stomach is the friend. It is digesting and distributing the energy to all the limbs of the body. Is it not?

Bob: It is so.

Śrīla Prabhupāda: Similarly, the central stomach of the whole creation is God, or Kṛṣṇa. He is the enjoyer, He is the friend, and, as the supreme proprietor, He is maintaining everyone. Just as a king can maintain the whole country's citizens because he is the proprietor. Without being the proprietor, how can one become everyone's friend? So these things have to be understood: Kṛṣṇa is the enjoyer, Kṛṣṇa is the proprietor, and Kṛṣṇa is the friend. If you know these three things, then your knowledge is full; you do not require to understand anything more. *Yasmin vijñāte sarvam evaṁ vijñātaṁ bhavati:* If you simply understand Kṛṣṇa by these three formulas, then your knowledge is complete. You don't require any more knowledge. But people will not agree. "Why should Kṛṣṇa be the proprietor? Hitler should be the proprietor. Or Nixon . . ." That is going on. Therefore you are in trouble. But if you understand these three things only, then your knowledge is complete. But we will not accept. We put forward so many impediments to understanding these three things, and that is the cause of our trouble. But in the *Bhagavad-gītā* it is plainly said:

bhoktāraṁ yajña-tapasāṁ
sarva-loka-maheśvaram
suhṛdaṁ sarva-bhūtānāṁ
jñātvā māṁ śāntim ṛcchati

["A person in full consciousness of Me, knowing Me as the

ultimate beneficiary of all sacrifices and austerities, the Supreme Lord of all planets and demigods and the benefactor and well-wisher of all living entities, attains peace from the pangs of material miseries."] But we won't take this. We put forward so many false proprietors, false friends, false enjoyers, and they fight one another. This is the situation of the world. If education is given and people take this knowledge, there is immediately peace (*śāntim ṛcchati*). This is knowledge, and if anyone follows this principle, he is honest. He does not claim, "It is mine." He knows everything: "Oh, it is Kṛṣṇa's, so therefore everything should be utilised for Kṛṣṇa's service." That is honesty. If this pencil belongs to me, the etiquette is for my students to ask, "Can I use this pencil?" Then I will reply, "Yes, you can."

Similarly, if I know that everything belongs to Kṛṣṇa, I will not use anything without His permission. That is honesty. And that is knowledge. One who does not know is ignorant; he is foolish. And a foolish man commits criminality. All criminals are foolish men. Out of ignorance one breaks the law. So ignorance is not bliss, but it is folly to be wise where ignorance is bliss. That is the difficulty. The whole world is enjoying ignorance. And when you talk about Kṛṣṇa consciousness, they do not appreciate it very much. If I say, "Kṛṣṇa is the proprietor; you are not the proprietor," you will not be very satisfied. Just see — ignorance is bliss.

So it is my foolishness to say the real truth. Therefore it is folly to be wise where ignorance is bliss. We are taking the risk of offending people, and they will think we are fools. If I say to a rich man, "You are not the proprietor. Kṛṣṇa is the proprietor, so whatever money you have, spend it for Kṛṣṇa," he will be angry. *Upadeśo hi mūrkhāṇāṁ prakopāya na śāntaye:* "If you instruct a rascal, he'll be angry." Therefore we go as beggars and say, "My dear sir, you are a very nice man. I am a *sannyāsī* beggar, and I want to construct a temple. Can you spare some money?" So he will think, "Oh, here is a beggar. Give him some money." But if I say, "Dear sir, you have millions of dollars at your disposal. That is Kṛṣṇa's money. Give it to me. I am Kṛṣṇa's servant." He will not be very satisfied. Rather, if I go as a beggar, he will give me something. And if I tell him the truth, he will not give me a farthing. We convince him as beggars. But we are not beggars; we are Kṛṣṇa's servants. We don't want anything from anyone, because we know Kṛṣṇa will provide everything. This is knowledge. For instance, a child will sometimes take something important, so we have to flatter him, "Oh, you are so nice. Please take these sweets and give me that paper. It is nothing; it is paper." And he will say, "Oh, yes. Take it. That's nice." And he gives the important paper back for two-penny sweets. So we have to do that. Why? Because a man will go to hell by taking Kṛṣṇa's money. So some way or other, take some money from him and engage him in the Kṛṣṇa consciousness movement.

Bob: And then he may not go to hell?

Śrīla Prabhupāda: Yes. You save him from going to hell. Because a farthing spent for Kṛṣṇa will be noted by Kṛṣṇa. This is called *ajñāta-sukṛti,* (spiritual activity one performs unknowingly). People in general are very poor in their thought; therefore the saintly persons move amongst them just to enlighten them a little, to give them a chance to serve Kṛṣṇa. That is the saintly person's duty. But if someone takes money from others and utilises it for his sense gratification, then he goes to hell. Then he is finished. He is a cheater, a criminal. You cannot take a farthing from anyone and use it for your own sense gratification.

Bob: I know people who are not Kṛṣṇa conscious, who are just slightly God conscious, but still these people are honest to the extent that they don't take from other people at all. And they try to be honest with other people.

Śrīla Prabhupāda: They do not take from other people, but they take from God.
Bob: So are these people half-good?
Śrīla Prabhupāda: Not good if they do not learn this principle — that God is the proprietor. What do you mean, "others' things"?
Bob: I'm thinking of poor people who need money and food but . . .
Śrīla Prabhupāda: Everyone needs money. Everyone needs it. Who is not poor? Who is not in need of money and food? You are also in need of money. So how do you distinguish poor from rich? Everyone needs money. If your definition is one who needs money and food, then everyone needs money and food. So everyone is poor.
Bob: I was thinking in terms of people who are relatively poor.
Śrīla Prabhupāda: Relatively, maybe. You are more hungry than me. That does not mean you are not hungry or that I am not hungry. I do not feel hungry now. That does not mean I do not ever feel hungry or I am not hungry. For the time being you may not be hungry. But tomorrow you'll be hungry.
Bob: What I feel is that somehow, although everybody around these people may be stealing, they still stand up and don't steal. Somehow they deserve something good to happen to them.
Śrīla Prabhupāda: The man who is thinking that he is not stealing is also a thief because he does not know that everything belongs to Kṛṣṇa. Therefore, whatever he is accepting, he is stealing.
Bob: Is he less of a thief?
Śrīla Prabhupāda: You may not know that I am the proprietor of this wrapper, but if you take it away, are you not stealing?

Bob: But maybe if I know it is yours and I take it, I am a worse thief than if I do not know whose it is. I just think it may be nobody's, so I take it.

Śrīla Prabhupāda: That is also stealing, because it must belong to somebody, and you are taking it without his permission. You may not know exactly who the proprietor is, but you know it must belong to someone. That is knowledge. Sometimes we see on the road so many valuable things left there: government property for repairing roads or some electrical work. A man may think, "Oh, fortunately these things are lying here, so I may take them." Is it not stealing?

Bob: It is stealing.

Śrīla Prabhupāda: Yes. He does not know that this is all government property, so he takes it away. That is stealing. And when he is caught, he is arrested and punished. So, similarly, whatever you are collecting . . . Suppose you are drinking a glass of water from the river, is the river your property?

Bob: No.

Śrīla Prabhupāda: Then? It is stealing. You have not created the river. You do not know who is the proprietor, but it is not your property. So, even if you drink a glass of water without knowing to whom it belongs, you are a thief. So you may think, "I am honest," but actually you are a thief. You must remember Kṛṣṇa. "Oh, Kṛṣṇa, it is Your creation, so kindly allow me to drink." This is honesty. Therefore a devotee always thinks of Kṛṣṇa. In all activities he thinks, "Oh, it is Kṛṣṇa's." This is honesty. So without Kṛṣṇa consciousness, everyone is a rascal, a thief, a rogue and a robber. These are their qualifications. Therefore, our conclusion is that anyone who does not understand Kṛṣṇa has no good qualifications. He is not honest, nor does he have any knowledge. Therefore he is a third-class man. Is that not correct? This is not dogmatism. This is a fact. So, you have understood what is knowledge and what is honesty?

Bob: In a way.
Śrīla Prabhupāda: Is there any other way? Defy it! Is there an alternative? We do not say anything that can be defied by anyone; that experience we have. Rather, we defy everyone: "Any questions?" Till now, Kṛṣṇa has given us protection. In public meetings in foreign countries, after speaking I ask, "Any questions?"
Bob: Now, I have none.
Śrīla Prabhupāda: In London, we had twelve days' lectures in Conway Hall. So after every meeting I was asking, "Any questions?"
Bob: Did you get many questions?
Śrīla Prabhupāda: Oh, yes, many. But some were foolish.
Bob: Let me ask one more question. What is being foolish?
Śrīla Prabhupāda: One having no knowledge is to be considered foolish.
Indian Gentleman: Some time ago in Calcutta they observed a week named, "Prevention of Cruelty to Animals Week".
Śrīla Prabhupāda: This is another foolishness. They are advertising prevention of cruelty, and they are maintaining thousands of slaughterhouses. You see? That is another foolishness. They are regularly cruel to animals, and they are making a society to prevent it. It is as if a gang of thieves calls itself "Goodman and Company".
Indian Gentleman: So I wanted just to ask —
Śrīla Prabhupāda: Before you ask, I'll give you the answer. Their philosophy is that when an animal is not properly nourished, that is cruelty. Therefore, instead of allowing it to starve, better to kill it. That is their theory. Is it not?
Bob: Yes.
Śrīla Prabhupāda: They say, "Oh, it is better to kill him than to give him so much pain." That theory is coming in communist countries. An old man, a grandfather, may be suffering,

so better to kill him. In Africa there is a class of men who make a festival by killing their great-grandfathers.
Śyāmasundara: They eat them?
Śrīla Prabhupāda: Yes.
A Devotee: My uncle and aunt could not take their dog overseas with them. So they said, "The poor dog will be so heartbroken without us." So they put him to sleep, killed him.
Śrīla Prabhupāda: Even Gandhi once killed a calf or cow because it was suffering very much. Gandhi ordered, "Instead of letting it suffer, just kill it."
Girirāja: Yesterday you said that the spiritual master may have to suffer due to the sinful activities of his disciples. What do you mean by sinful activities?
Śrīla Prabhupāda: At initiation you promise, "I shall follow the regulative principles." If you do not follow, that is sinful. Very simple. You break the promise and do nasty things; then you are sinful. Is it not?
Girirāja: Yes. But there are some things that although we're instructed to do, and even though we try to do, we cannot yet do perfectly.
Śrīla Prabhupāda: You try to do and cannot do? How is that?
Girirāja: Like chanting attentively. Sometimes we try to, but . . .
Śrīla Prabhupāda: Well, that is not a fault. Suppose you are trying to do something, but due to your inexperience you sometimes fail. That is not a fault. You are trying. There is a verse in the *Bhāgavatam* that if a devotee is trying his best but due to his incapability he sometimes fails, Kṛṣṇa excuses him. And in the *Bhagavad-gītā* also it is said, *api cet sudurācāro bhajate mām ananya-bhāk.* Sometimes one does something nonsensical unwillingly, due to past bad habits because

habit is second nature. But that does not mean he is faulty. Still he must repent that he has done this. And he should try to avoid it as far as possible. But habit is second nature. Sometimes, in spite of your trying hard, *māyā* is so strong that it pushes with pitfalls. That can be excused. Kṛṣṇa does excuse. But those who are doing something willingly are not excused. If I think that because I am chanting, I may therefore commit all this nonsense and it will be nullified, that is the greatest offence.

EIGHT

Advancing in Kṛṣṇa Consciousness (an exchange of letters)

Springfield, New Jersey
June 12, 1972

Dear Prabhupāda,

I offer my humble obeisances.

I have been associating with the devotees of the New York temple. With the association of such fine, advanced devotees, I hope that I may make some advancement in Kṛṣṇa consciousness. My fiancée has started to come to the temple and is chanting a little. She knew nothing about Kṛṣṇa consciousness until I wrote her about it from India. Atreya Ṛṣi has been kind enough to invite us to his home so that we may see a good example of householder life.

I went to Bombay the end of April for discharge from the Peace Corps. I was fortunate enough to come down with a minor illness, so I had to stay in Bombay for two weeks. I spent the time with the advanced and kind devotees at Juhu. Unfortunately you had left five days previously.

I understand so little, but I have faith in the process of Kṛṣṇa consciousness and hope to take to it more and more.

I hope that I may personally hear you in New York.

Thank you for the kindness you have shown to a very undeserving boy.

Sincerely,
Bob Cohen

A.C. Bhaktivedanta Swami
ISKCON Los Angeles
June 16, 1972

Bob Cohen
Springfield, New Jersey

My dear Bob,

Please accept my blessings. I thank you very much for your letter dated June 12, 1972. I have noted the sentiments expressed therein with great pleasure. I am very glad to hear that you are associating with us. I know that you are a very good boy, very intelligent, and your behaviour is gentle, so I have all confidence that very quickly Kṛṣṇa will bestow all His blessings upon you, and you will feel yourself becoming perfectly happy in Kṛṣṇa consciousness. One makes his advancement in Kṛṣṇa consciousness by voluntarily giving up his attachment to material nature, or *māyā.* Such renunciation is called *tapasya.* But we are not very willing to perform austerities without good reason; therefore any man with a good scientific and philosophical mind, like your good self, must first appreciate what transcendental knowledge is. If you get knowledge, automatically *tapasya* will follow, and then you make your advancement in spiritual life. So to get knowledge is the first item for anyone who is hoping to find the perfection of his life. Therefore I advise you to read our books daily as far as possible and try to understand the subject matter from different angles of vision by discussing it frequently with the devotees at the New York temple. In this way you will gradually become convinced, and by your sincere attitude and devotional service you will make progress.

Yes, having some faith in me and in this Kṛṣṇa consciousness process is the first and only requirement for getting actual wisdom. If there is faith, understanding will follow. And as your understanding increases, so will your disgust with the spell of illusory energy. And when you voluntarily give up your entanglements in the material world, then the progress is assured.

I think we are just now typing up the tapes of those conversations we held in Māyāpur, and we shall be publishing them as a book. It will be called *Perfect Questions, Perfect Answers.* I shall send you a copy as soon as they are ready to distribute. Meanwhile, I shall be stopping in New York for two or three days on my way to London for the Ratha-yātrā festival there. I am not yet certain when I shall be arriving in New York, but it will be some time in the early part of July. You may keep in regular contact with Bali Mardana regarding the arrival date, and I shall be very much engladdened to meet with you in New York once again. Again we shall discuss if you have any questions.

Hoping this will meet you in good health and a happy mood,

Your ever well-wisher,
A.C. Bhaktivedanta Swami

NINE

Deciding for the Future
New York — July 4, 1972

Bob: I received your very kind letter about a week ago.
Śrīla Prabhupāda: You are a very intelligent boy. Try to understand this philosophy. It is very important. People are wasting so much energy for sense gratification. They are not aware of what is going to happen in the next life. There is a next life, but foolish people are ignorant. This life is preparation for the next life. That they do not know. The modern education and its universities are completely in darkness about this simple knowledge. We are changing bodies every moment — that is a medical fact. After leaving this body, we will have to accept another body. How are we going to accept that body? What kind of body? This can also be known. For example, if someone is being educated, one can understand that when he passes his examination, he is going to be an engineer or medical practitioner. Similarly, in this life, you can prepare yourself to become something in the next life.
Barbara [*Bob's wife*]: Can we decide what we want to be next life?
Śrīla Prabhupāda: Yes, you can decide. We have decided that next life we are going to Kṛṣṇa. This is our decision — to go back home, back to Godhead. Suppose you want to

become an engineer or a medical practitioner. With that objective in mind you prepare and educate yourself. Similarly, you can decide what you are going to do next life. But if you don't decide, then material nature will decide for you.
Barbara: Could I have been Kṛṣṇa conscious in my last life? Is it possible that I was a Kṛṣṇa devotee in my last life who has come back again?
Śrīla Prabhupāda: It doesn't matter whether you were or you weren't. But you can become now. Take advantage of our Kṛṣṇa consciousness movement. When one is perfectly Kṛṣṇa's devotee, he does not come back. But if there is a little deficiency, then there is a possibility of coming back. But even though there is a deficiency, a devotee comes back to a nice family. *Śucīnāṁ śrīmatāṁ gehe yoga-bhraṣṭo 'bhijāyate.* ["The unsuccessful *yogī* takes birth in a religious or aristocratic family."] So human intelligence can decide for the future. But an animal cannot decide. We have discriminatory power. If I do this, I will be benefited; if I do that, I will not be benefited. This is there in human life. So you have to use it properly. You should know what is the goal of life and decide in that way. That is human civilisation.
Barbara: Have you ever seen Kṛṣṇa?
Śrīla Prabhupāda: Yes.
Barbara: You have?
Śrīla Prabhupāda: Daily. Every moment.
Barbara: But not in the material body?
Śrīla Prabhupāda: He has no material body.
Barbara: Well, they have pictures of Kṛṣṇa in the temple.
Śrīla Prabhupāda: That is not a material body. You are seeing materially because you have material eyes. Because you have material eyes, you cannot see the spiritual form. Therefore Kṛṣṇa kindly appears to be in a material body so that you can see. Just because He has kindly made Himself fit

for your seeing, that does not mean He has a material body. Suppose the President of the United States kindly comes to your house. That does not mean that his position and your position are the same. It is his kindness. Out of love, he may come to your house, but that does not mean he is on the same level as you. Similarly, because we cannot see Kṛṣṇa with our present eyes, He therefore appears before us as a painting, as made of stone or as made of wood. Kṛṣṇa is not different from these paintings and wood because everything is Kṛṣṇa.

Barbara: What happens to our spirit after we die?

Śrīla Prabhupāda: You get another body.

Barbara: Immediately?

Śrīla Prabhupāda: Yes. Just as when you change your flat: you fix up your new flat first; then you leave your present one and go there.

Barbara: So do we know what type of body we will get?

Śrīla Prabhupāda: Yes, provided you are qualified. But for those who do not know, nature will arrange things. If you do not know, this means you have not prepared your life. So incidentally, at the time of death, your mentality will create another body, and nature will supply it.

Bob: Prabhupāda, some religious people claim that Jesus is guiding them. Can this be so?

Śrīla Prabhupāda: Yes, but they are not taking the guidance. Jesus is guiding the Christians, telling them, "Thou shalt not kill;" but they are killing. So where is Jesus' guidance? Simply saying, "I am guided by Jesus Christ. But I don't care for his words." Is that guidance? Will that do? Therefore, nobody is being guided by Jesus Christ. Their claim is false. It is very hard to find a man who is actually being guided by Jesus Christ. Jesus Christ's guidance is available, but nobody is caring for him. They have taken Jesus Christ as a contractor to take up their sins. That is their philosophy.

They commit all kinds of sins, and poor Jesus Christ will be responsible; that is their religion. Therefore they say, "We have a very good religion: for all our sinful activities, Jesus Christ will die." Is that good religion? They have no sympathy for Jesus Christ. He died for our sins. Why should we commit sins again? Such a great life has been sacrificed for our sins; we should be guided by Jesus Christ. But if you take it otherwise and say, "Ah, I shall go on committing all sins, and Jesus Christ will make a contract to nullify them. Then I'll simply go to church, confess and then come back to do all nonsense again." Do you think that shows very good intelligence?

Bob: No.

Śrīla Prabhupāda: One who is genuinely guided by Jesus Christ will certainly get liberation. But it is very hard to find a man who is actually being guided by Jesus Christ.

Bob: What about the "Jesus freaks," young people who read the Bible very often?

Śrīla Prabhupāda: But violence is against the Bible's injunctions. How can they kill if they are following the Bible?

Bob: They claim that the Bible says Jesus ate meat.

Śrīla Prabhupāda: That's all right. He may eat anything; he is powerful. But he has ordered, "Thou shalt not kill. You must stop killing." He can eat the whole world. But you cannot compare us to him. You cannot imitate Jesus Christ; you have to abide by his order. Then you are guided by Jesus Christ. That is actual obedience. It is explained in the *Bhāgavatam* that one who is *īśvara,* who is empowered, can do anything. But we cannot imitate. We have to abide by his order. "I will do what he tells me."

Admitting that Jesus Christ may have eaten meat, you do not know under what conditions. He was advising others not to kill, yet he was eating meat himself. Do you think that Jesus Christ was contradicting himself?

Bob: No.

Śrīla Prabhupāda: That is real faith in him; that he cannot do that. So why has he eaten meat? He knows why, but he has asked me not to kill. I have to follow. That is the real system. You are not Jesus Christ; you cannot imitate him. He has sacrificed his life for God. Can you do that? Why only imitate Jesus Christ by eating meat? Why not imitate him by sacrificing your life for spreading God consciousness? They are so-called Christians, yet what are they doing for God? Consider how the sun is absorbing urine. But can you drink urine? If you want to imitate the sun and drink urine; can you? Jesus Christ is powerful; he can do everything. But we cannot imitate; we simply have to abide by his order. That is real Christianity. It is wrong to imitate a powerful man.

The *Vedas* describe how there was once an ocean of poison and no one knew what to do with it. Then Lord Śiva said, "All right, I'll drink it." So he drank the whole poison ocean and kept it in his throat. Now, can you drink poison? Not the whole ocean, but just one cup? Lord Śiva never advised that we drink poison, how can we imitate him? You have to abide by the advice, not imitate. These LSD and marijuana people say that Lord Śiva used to smoke *gañja* [hashish]. But Lord Śiva drank the whole poisoned ocean. Can you do that?

It is Lord Śiva's *instructions* that should be taken. When he was asked by Pārvatī what method of worship is best, he said, "The best worship is worship of Lord Viṣṇu, Kṛṣṇa." *Viṣṇor ārādhanaṁ param.* There are many demigods, but he recommended Viṣṇu worship as the best. And then he said, "Even better than Viṣṇu worship is worship of a Vaiṣṇava." *Tadīyānām* — His servants, or those who are in relation to Him. For instance, we worship the *tulasī* plant. We are not worshipping all plants, but because *tulasī* has a very intimate connection with Kṛṣṇa, Viṣṇu, we are worshiping her. Similarly, if anything is intimately related to Kṛṣṇa, worship of that thing is better than worship of Viṣṇu.

Bob: Why is that?

Śrīla Prabhupāda: Because Kṛṣṇa will be pleased. Suppose a friend pats your dog. "My, what a nice dog you have." You become pleased: "Oh, he is my good friend." [*Some Indian guests enter the room.*]

Śrīla Prabhupāda: Please have some *prasādam.*

[*Śrīla Prabhupāda continues speaking with his guests in English and Hindi. It is his last day in New York, and his plane to London is scheduled to leave in only a few hours. Bob has brought a car to drive Śrīla Prabhupāda to Kennedy Airport. The devotees are scurrying about, bringing luggage to the car, putting manuscripts of Śrīla Prabhupāda's latest translating work in order and making other last-minute arrangements.*]

Śyāmasundara: Everything's ready, Śrīla Prabhupāda. The car is waiting for us.

Śrīla Prabhupāda: So? We can go now? All right. Hare Kṛṣṇa!

Concluding Words

On July 19, 1976, His Divine Grace Śrīla Prabhupāda accepted my wife and me as his disciples and initiated us with the names Bhakti-devi dasi and Brahmatīrtha dāsa. As I reflect back on that day, I can see how fortunate I was to have met His Divine Grace and my Godbrothers in the Hare Kṛṣṇa movement.

When I was handed my beads at initiation, I promised to follow the regulative principles and to chant God's names daily. Four years previously, Śrīla Prabhupāda had advised me to follow these principles. He said that within six months I could be like the other devotees; all unnecessary things (*anarthas*), such as mundane movies and restaurants, would cease to attract me. "The whole human life is meant for purification," he said. I was interested in being purified, even though I did not really know what purification meant. I had gone to India with the Peace Corps hoping to find a higher level of consciousness. I did not believe that satisfying the senses was the all in all, yet I myself was bound by the senses. Later I could understand that yoga means becoming free from the dictation of the senses.

Upon returning to America, I started graduate school in geology, got married, and became somewhat entangled in domestic responsibilities, but I would very often think of my conversations with Śrīla Prabhupāda and of his instructions. One of his primary instructions was simply to associate with the devotees, and this I gladly did. Devotees are different: by understanding that loving service to the Supreme Lord is the goal of life, they avoid getting caught up in the petty affairs of sense gratification and false ego.

Visiting the temple was most refreshing. Gradually, my wife and I became friends with many devotees and wanted somehow to do some service for the movement. I sponsored a *Bhakti-yoga* Club at the University, and our apartment served as a way station for travelling parties of devotees.

As we followed Śrīla Prabhupāda's instructions, even our eating became purified. In India I had told Śrīla Prabhupāda that I could not offer my food as the devotees do because I did not understand that Kṛṣṇa is God. So he told me simply to thank God for my food before eating. This we did, and finally our devotion matured, and we started offering our food to the Supreme Lord. What a wonderful feeling, to be cooking for the Supreme Lord! This actually freed us from the control of the tongue.

Finally, we were ready to become fully involved in temple life. By Kṛṣṇa's grace, I obtained a job near a temple in Texas and began to take part in all the temple programmes. In this way, all the *anarthas* disappeared, just as Śrīla Prabhupāda had predicted. It was like having a burden lifted from our shoulders. We were no longer servants of our senses, but servants of God and His devotees. The value of Śrīla Prabhupāda's instructions had become clear. A human being is not meant to labour like an ass and enjoy like a dog. Purification means coming to a higher level of consciousness.

Even though I have been initiated, I still admire my Godbrothers' spiritual awareness and desire to advance. Actually, initiation is just the beginning.

Brahmatīrtha dāsa Adhikārī
(Bob Cohen)

Houston, Texas
October 16, 1976

His Divine Grace A.C. Bhaktivedanta Swami Prabhupāda

His Divine Grace A.C. Bhaktivedanta Swami Prabhupāda appeared in this world in 1896 in Calcutta, India. He first met his spiritual master, Śrīla Bhaktisiddhānta Sarasvatī Gosvāmī, in Calcutta in 1922. Bhaktisiddhānta Sarasvatī was a prominent religious scholar and the founder of the Gauḍīya Maṭha (a *Vaiṣṇava* movement with sixty-four centres) in India. He liked this educated young man and convinced him to dedicate his life to teaching Vedic knowledge. Śrīla Prabhupāda became his student and, in 1933, received initiation as his disciple.

At their first meeting Śrīla Bhaktisiddhānta Sarasvatī requested Śrīla Prabhupāda to broadcast Vedic knowledge in English. In the years that followed, Śrīla Prabhupāda wrote a commentary on the *Bhagavad-gītā* and assisted the Gauḍīya Maṭha in its work. In 1944, he started *Back to Godhead*, a fortnightly magazine in English. Singlehandedly, Śrīla Prabhupāda edited it, typed the manuscripts, checked the galley proofs, and even distributed the individual copies. The magazine now continues to be published by his disciples throughout the world in different languages.

In 1950 Śrīla Prabhupāda retired from domestic life to devote more time to his studies and writing. He travelled to the holy town of Vṛndāvana, where he lived in humble circumstances in the historic temple of Rādhā-Dāmodara. There, for several years, he engaged in deep study and writing. He accepted the renounced order of life (*sannyāsa*) in 1959.

It was at the Rādhā-Dāmodara temple that Śrīla Prabhupāda began to work on his life's masterpiece: a multivolume translation of the eighteen-thousand verse *Śrīmad-Bhāgavatam* (*Bhāgavata Purāṇa*) with full commentary. After publishing three volumes of the *Bhāgavatam*, Śrīla Prabhupāda travelled by freighter to New York City. He was practically penniless, but had faith that the mission of his spiritual master could be successful. On the day he landed in America and saw the grey mists hanging over the towering skyscrapers, he penned these words in his diary: "My dear Lord Kṛṣṇa, I am sure that when this transcendental message penetrates their hearts, they will certainly feel gladdened and thus become liberated from all unhappy conditions of life." He was sixty-nine years old, alone and with few resources, but the wealth of spiritual knowledge and devotion he possessed was an unwavering source of strength and inspiration.

"At a very advanced age, when most people would be resting on their laurels," writes Harvey Cox, Harvard University theologian and author, "Śrīla Prabhupāda harkened to the mandate of his own spiritual teacher and set out on the difficult and demanding voyage to America. Śrīla Prabhupāda is, of course, only one of thousands of teachers. But in another sense, he is one in a thousand, maybe one in a million."

In 1966, Śrīla Prabhupāda founded the International Society for Krishna Consciousness, which became the formal name for the Hare Kṛṣṇa Movement.

In the years that followed, Śrīla Prabhupāda gradually attracted tens of thousands of followers, started more than a hundred temples and *āśramas*, and published scores of books. His achievement is remarkable in that he transplanted India's ancient spiritual culture to the twentieth-century Western world.

In 1968, Śrīla Prabhupāda sent three devotee couples to bring Kṛṣṇa consciousness to the U.K. At first, these devotees were cared for by Hindu families who appreciated their mission, but soon they became well known in London for the street-chanting on Oxford Street. A headline in the *Times* announced, "Kṛṣṇa Chant Startles London". But the *mahā-mantra* soon became popular. Former Beatle, George Harrison, who had known Śrīla Prabhupāda and the chanting before the devotees came to England, wanted to help. He arranged to produce a recording of the *mantra* on the Beatles' Apple label. It reached the Top Ten in Britain and number one in some other countries.

When Śrīla Prabhupāda arrived in England, he was the guest of John Lennon at his estate in Tittenhurst, while work was progressing on the temple in Bloomsbury, near the British Museum. In November 1969, Śrīla Prabhupāda opened the temple — the first Rādhā-Kṛṣṇa temple in Europe. The movement grew from strength to strength. Once again, George Harrison offered to help by donating a beautiful mock-Tudor manor house and estate in Hertfordshire. Now named Bhaktivedanta Manor, it is the Society's main training centre in Britain.

New devotees of Kṛṣṇa soon became highly visible in all the major cities around the world by their public chanting and their distribution of Śrīla Prabhupāda's books of Vedic knowledge. They began staging joyous cultural festivals throughout the year and serving millions of plates of delicious food offered to Kṛṣṇa (known as *prasādam*) throughout the world. As a result, ISKCON has significantly influenced the lives of hundreds of thousands of people. The late A.L. Basham, one of the world's leading authorities on Indian history and culture, wrote, "The Hare Kṛṣṇa movement arose out of next to nothing in less than twenty years and has become known all over the West. This is an important fact in the history of the Western world."

In just twelve years, despite his advanced age, Śrīla Prabhupāda circled the globe fourteen times on lecture tours that took him to six continents. Yet this vigorous schedule did not slow his prolific literary output. His writings constitute a veritable library of Vedic philosophy, religion, literature, and culture.

Indeed, Śrīla Prabhupāda's most significant contribution is his books. Highly respected by academics for their authority, depth and clarity, they are used as textbooks in numerous university courses.

Garry Gelade, a professor at Oxford University's Department of Philosophy, wrote of them: "These texts are to be treasured. No one of whatever faith or philosophical persuasion who reads these books with an open mind can fail to be moved and impressed." And Dr. Larry Shinn, Dean of the College of Arts and Sciences at Bucknell University, wrote, "Prabhupāda's personal piety gave him real authority. He exhibited complete command of the scriptures, and unusual depth of realization, and an outstanding personal example, because he actually lived what he taught."

His writings have been translated into over 50 languages. The Bhaktivedanta Book Trust, established in 1972 to publish the works of Śrīla Prabhupāda, has thus become the world's largest publisher of books in the field of Indian religion and philosophy. 450 million copies in over 50 languages had been sold by the end of 1991.

Before he passed away on the 14th of November 1977 he had guided that Society and seen it grow to a world-wide confederation of more than one hundred *āśramas*, schools, temples, institutes, and farm communities.

Glossary

Ācārya—a spiritual master who teaches by example.
Ārati—a ceremony for greeting the Lord with offerings of food, lamps, fans, flowers and incense.
Arcanā—the devotional practice of Deity worship.
Āśrama—a spiritual order of life.
Asuras—atheistic demons.
Avatāra—a descent of the Supreme Lord.

Bhagavad-gītā—the basic directions for spiritual life spoken by the Lord Himself.
Bhakta—a devotee.
Bhakti-yoga—linking with the Supreme Lord in ecstatic devotional service.
Brahmacarya—celibate student life; the first order of Vedic spiritual life.
Brahman—the Absolute Truth; especially, the impersonal aspect of the Absolute.
Brāhmaṇa—a person in the mode of goodness; first Vedic social order.

Dharma—eternal occupational duty; religious principles.

Ekādaśī—a special fast day for increased remembrance of Kṛṣṇa, which comes on the eleventh day of both the waxing and waning moon.

Goloka (Kṛṣṇaloka)—the highest spiritual planet, containing Kṛṣṇa's personal abodes, Dvārakā, Mathurā and Vṛndāvana.

Gopīs—Kṛṣṇa's cowherd girl friends who are His most confidential servitors.

Gṛhastha—regulated householder life; the second order of Vedic spiritual life.

Guru—a spiritual master or superior person.

Hare Kṛṣṇa *mantra*—*See: Mahā-mantra*

Jīva-tattva—the living entities, who are small parts of the Lord.

Kali-yuga (Age of Kali)—the present age, which is characterized by quarrel. It is last in the cycle of four, and began five thousand years ago.

Karatālas—hand cymbals used in *kīrtana.*

Karma—fruitive action, for which there is always reaction, good or bad.

Karmī—one who is satisfied with working hard for flickering sense gratification.

Kīrtana—chanting the glories of the Supreme Lord.

Kṛṣṇaloka—*See:* Goloka

Kṣatriyas—a warrior or administrator; the second Vedic social order.

Mahā-mantra—the great chanting for deliverance: Hare Kṛṣṇa, Hare Kṛṣṇa, Kṛṣṇa Kṛṣṇa, Hare Hare/ Hare Rāma, Hare Rāma, Rāma Rāma, Hare Hare.

Mantra—a sound vibration that can deliver the mind from illusion.

Mathurā—Lord Kṛṣṇa's abode, surrounding Vṛndāvana, where He took birth and later returned to after performing His Vṛndāvana pastimes.

Māyā—(*mā*—not; *yā*—this), illusion; forgetfulness of one's relationship with Kṛṣṇa.

Māyāvādīs—impersonal philosophers who say that the Lord cannot have a transcendental body.

Mṛdaṅga—a clay drum used for congregational chanting.

Paramparā—the chain of spiritual masters in disciplic succession.

Prasāda—food spiritualized by being offered to the Lord.

Sac-cid-ānanda-vigraha—the Lord's transcendental form, which is eternal, full of knowledge and bliss.

Saṅkīrtana—public chanting of the names of God, the approved *yoga* process for this age.

Sannyāsa—renounced life; the fourth order of Vedic spiritual life.

Śāstras—revealed scriptures.

Śravaṇaṁ kīrtanaṁ viṣṇoḥ—the devotional processes of hearing and chanting about Lord Viṣṇu.

Śūdra—a laborer; the fourth of the Vedic social orders.

Svāmī—one who controls his mind and senses; title of one in the renounced order of life.

Tapasya—austerity; accepting voluntary inconvenience for a higher purpose.

Tilaka—auspicious clay marks that sanctify a devotee's body as a temple of the Lord.

Vaikuṇṭha—the spiritual world, where there is no anxiety.

Vaiṣṇava—a devotee of Lord Viṣṇu, or Kṛṣṇa.

Vaiśyas—farmers and merchants; the third Vedic social order.

Vānaprastha—one who has retired from family life; the third order of Vedic spiritual life.

Varṇāśrama—the Vedic social system of four social and four spiritual orders.

Vedas—the original revealed scriptures, first spoken by the Lord Himself.

Viṣṇu, Lord—Kṛṣṇa's first expansion for the creation and maintenance of the material universes.

Vṛndāvana—Kṛṣṇa's personal abode, where He fully manifests His quality of sweetness.

Vyāsadeva—Kṛṣṇa's incarnation, at the end of Dvāpara-yuga, for compiling the *Vedas*.

Yajña—sacrifice, work done for the satisfaction of Lord Viṣṇu.

Yogī—a transcendentalist who, in one way or another, is striving for union with the Supreme.

Yuga—ages in the life of a universe, occurring in a repeated cycle of four.

Centres of the International Society for Krishna Consciousness

Founder-*Ācārya:* His Divine Grace
A.C. Bhaktivedanta Swami Prabhupāda

August 1993

"For further information of classes, programmes, festivals or residential courses, please contact your local centre. There may be other meetings held locally. Please contact the centre nearest you."

UNITED KINGDOM AND IRELAND

Belfast, Northern Ireland – Brookland, 140 Upper Dunmurray Lane, BT17 OHE/ Tel. +44 (0232) 620530

Birmingham, West Midlands – 84 Stanmore Rd., Edgbaston, B16 9TB/ Tel. +44 (021) 420-4999

Dublin, Ireland – Hare Krishna Centre, 56 Dame St., Dublin 2/ Tel. +353 (1) 6791306

Leicester, England – 21 Thoresby St., North Evington, Leicester LE5 4GU/ Tel. +44 (0533) 762587

Liverpool, England – 114 Bold Street, L1 4HY/ Tel. +44 (051) 708-9400

London, England (city) – Sri Sri Radha Krishna Temple, 10 Soho St., London W1V 5DA/ Tel. +44 (071) 4373662

London, England (country) – Bhaktivedanta Manor, Letchmore Heath, Watford, Hertfordshire WD2 8EP/ Tel. +44 (0923) 857244

Manchester, England – 20 Mayfield Rd., Whalley Range, Manchester M16 8FT/ Tel. +44 (061) 2264416

Newcastle upon Tyne, England – Hare Krishna Centre, 21 Leazes Park Rd., NE1 4PF/ Tel. +44 (091) 2220150

Scotland – Karuna Bhavan, Bankhouse Road, Lesmahagow, Lanarkshire ML11 9PT/ Tel. +44 (0555) 894790

FARM COMMUNITIES

Lisnaskea, North Ireland – Lake Island of Inis Rath, Lisnaskea Co. Fermanagh/ Tel. +44 (03657) 21512

London, England–(contact Bhaktivedanta Manor)

RESTAURANT

London, England–Govinda's, 10 Soho St./ Tel. +44 (071) 4373662

Manchester, England–Govinda's, 244 Deansgate/ Tel. +44 (061) 834- 9197

Kṛṣṇa conscious programmes are held regularly in more than twenty other cities in the U.K. For information, contact Bhaktivedanta Books Ltd., Reader Services Dept., P.O. Box 324, Borehamwood, Herts WD6 1NB/ Tel. (081) 9051244.

NORTH AMERICA

CANADA

Montreal, Quebec–1626 Pie IX Boulevard, H1V 2C5/ Tel. +1 (514) 521-1301

Ottawa, Ontario–212 Somerset St. E., K1N 6V4/ Tel. +1 (613) 565-6544

Regina, Saskatchewan–1279 Retallack St., S4T 2H8/ Tel. +1 (306) 525-1640

Toronto, Ontario–243 Avenue Rd., M5R 2J6/ Tel. +1 (416) 922-5415

Vancouver, B.C.–5462 S.E. Marine Dr., Burnaby V5J 3G8/ Tel. +1 (604) 433-9728

FARM COMMUNITY

Ashcroft, B.C.–Saranagati Dhama, Box 99, Ashcroft, B.C. V0K 1A0

RESTAURANTS

Hamilton, Ontario–Govinda's, 195 Locke St. South, L8T 4B5/ Tel. +1 (416) 523-6209

Ottawa–(at ISKCON Ottawa)

Toronto–Hare Krishna Dining Room (at ISKCON Toronto)

Vancouver–Hare Krishna Buffet (at ISKCON Vancouver)

Vancouver–The Hare Krishna Place, 46 Begbie St., New Westminster

U.S.A.

Atlanta, Georgia–1287 South Ponce de Leon Ave. N.E., 30306/ Tel. +1 (404) 378-9234

Baltimore, Maryland–200 Bloomsbury Ave., Catonsville, 21228/ Tel. +1 (410) 744-1624 or 4069

Boise, Idaho–1615 Martha St., 83706/ Tel. +1 (208) 344-4274

Boston, Massachusetts–72 Commonwealth Ave., 02116/ Tel. +1 (617) 247-8611

Boulder, Colorado–917 Pleasant St., 80302/ Tel. +1 (303) 444-7005

Chicago, Illinois–1716 W. Lunt Ave., 60626/ Tel. +1 (312) 973-0900

Cleveland, Ohio–11206 Clifton Blvd., 44102/ Tel. +1 (216) 651-6670

Dallas, Texas–5430 Gurley Ave. 75223/ Tel. +1 (214) 827-6330
Denver, Colorado–1400 Cherry St., 80220/ Tel. +1 (303) 333-5461
Detroit, Michigan–383 Lenox Ave., 48215/ Tel. +1 (313) 824-6000
Gainesville, Florida–214 N.W. 14th St., 32603/ Tel. +1 (904) 336-4183
Gurabo, Puerto Rico–Route 181, P.O. Box 8440 HC-01, 00778-9763/ Tel. (809) 737-5222
Hartford, Connecticut–1683 Main St., E. Hartford, 06108/ Tel. +1 (203) 289-7252
Honolulu, Hawaii–51 Coelho Way, 96817/ Tel. +1 (808) 595-3947
Houston, Texas–1320 W. 34th St., 77018/ Tel. +1 (713) 686-4482
Laguna Beach, California–285 Legion St. 92651/ Tel. +1 (714) 494-7029
Lansing, Michigan–1914 E. Michigan Ave. 48912/ Tel. +1 (517) 484-2209
Long Island, New York–197 S. Ocean Ave., Freeport, 11520/ Tel. +1 (516) 867-9045
Los Angeles, California–3764 Watseka Ave., 90034/ Tel. +1 (310) 836-2676
Miami, Florida–3220 Virginia St., 33133/ Tel. +1 (305) 442-7218
New Orleans, Louisiana–2936 Esplanade Ave., 70119/ Tel. +1 (504) 484-6084
New York, New York–305 Schermerhorn St., Brooklyn, 11217/ Tel. +1 (718) 855-6714
New York, New York–26 Second Avenue, 10003/ Tel. +1 (212) 420-8803
Philadelphia, Pennsylvania–51 West Allens Lane, 19119/ Tel. +1 (215) 247-4600
Philadelphia, Pennsylvania–529 South St., 19147/ Tel. +1 (215) 829-0077
St. Louis, Missouri–3926 Lindell Blvd., 63108/ Tel. +1 (314) 535-8085
San Diego, California–1030 Grand Ave., Pacific Beach, 92109/ Tel. +1 (619) 483-2500
San Francisco, California–84 Carl St., 94117/ Tel. +1 (415) 661-7320
San Francisco, California–2334 Stuart St., Berkeley, 94705/ Tel. +1 (510) 644-1113
Seattle, Washington–1420 228th Ave. S.E., Issaquah, 98027/ Tel. +1 (206) 391-3293
Tallahassee, Florida–1323 Nylic St. (mail: P.O. Box 20224, 32304)/ Tel. +1 (904) 681-9258
Topanga, California–20395 Callon Dr. 90290/ Tel. +1 (213) 455-1658
Towaco, New Jersey–(mail: P.O. Box 109, 07082)/ Tel. +1 (201) 299-0970
Tucson, Arizona–711 E. Blacklidge Dr., 85719/ Tel. +1 (602) 792-0630
Walla Walla, Washington–314 E. Poplar, 99362/ Tel. +1 (509) 525-7133
Washington, D.C.–10310 Oaklyn Dr., Potomac, Maryland 20854/ Tel. +1 (301) 299-2100

FARM COMMUNITIES

Alachua, Florida (New Ramana-reti)–Box 819, Alachua, 32615/ Tel. +1 (904) 462-2017
Carriere, Mississippi (New Talavan)–31492 Anner Road, 39426/ Tel. +1 (601) 798-6623
Gurabo, Puerto Rico (New Govardhana Hill)–(contact ISKCON Gurabo)

Hillsborough, North Carolina (New Goloka)–Rt. 6, Box 701, 27278/
Tel. (919) 732-6492

Mulberry, Tennessee (Murari-sevaka)–Rt. No. 1, Box 146-A, 37359/
Tel. (615) 759-6888

Port Royal, Pennsylvania (Gita Nagari)–R.D. No. 1, Box 839, 17082/
Tel. (717) 527-4101

RESTAURANTS AND DINING

Atlanta–The Hare Krishna Dinner Club (at ISKCON Atlanta)

Boise–Govinda's, 500 W. Main St./ Tel. +1 (208) 338-9710

Chicago–Govinda's Buffet (at ISKCON Chicago)

Dallas–Kalachandji's (at ISKCON Dallas)

Denver–Govinda's (at ISKCON Denver)

Detroit–Govinda's (at ISKCON Detroit)/ Tel. +1 (313) 331-6740

Eugene, Oregon–Govinda's Vegetarian Buffet, 270 W. 8th St., 97401/
Tel. +1 (503) 686-3531

Honolulu–Gauranga's Vegetarian Dining (at ISKCON Honolulu)

Laguna Beach, California–Gauranga's (at ISKCON Laguna Beach)

Lansing, Michigan–Govinda's Diners' Club (at ISKCON Lansing)

Los Angeles–Govinda's, 9624 Venice Blvd., Culver City, 90230/
Tel. +1 (310) 836-1269

Miami–(at ISKCON Miami)

Ojai, California–Govinda's Veggie Buffet, 1002 E. Ojai Ave., 93023/
Tel. +1 (805) 646-1133

Philadelphia–Govinda's, 521 South Street, 19147/ Tel. +1 (215) 829-0077

Provo, Utah–Govinda's Buffet, 260 North University, 84601/
Tel. +1 (801) 375-0404

St. Louis, Missouri–Govinda's (at ISCKON St. Louis)

San Diego–Govinda's at the Beach (at ISKCON San Diego)/
Tel. +1 (619) 483-5266

San Francisco–Govinda's (at ISKCON Berkeley)/ Tel. +1 (510) 644- 2777

AUSTRALASIA

AUSTRALIA

Adelaide–74 Semaphore Rd., Semaphore, S.A. 5019/
Tel. +61 (08) 493 200

Brisbane–95 Bank Rd., Graceville, Q.L.D. (mail: P.O. Box 83, Indooroopilly 4068)/ Tel. +61 (07) 379-5455

Canberra–P.O. Box 1411, Canberra ACT 2060/ Tel. +61 (06) 290-1869

Melbourne–197 Danks St., Albert Park, Victoria 3206 (mail: P.O. Box 125)/ Tel. +61 (03) 699-5122

Perth–144 Railway Parade (cnr. The Strand), Bayswater (mail: P.O. Box 102, Bayswater, W.A. 6053)/ Tel. +61 (09) 370-1552

Sydney–180 Falcon St., North Sydney, N.S.W. 2060 (mail: P. O. Box 459, Cammeray, N.S.W. 2062)/ Tel. +61 (02) 959-4558

FARM COMMUNITIES

Bambra (New Nandagram)–Oak Hill, Dean's Marsh Road, Bambra, VIC 3241/ Tel. +61 (052) 88-7383

Millfield, N.S.W.–New Gokula Farm, Lewis Lane (off Mt. View Rd. Millfield near Cessnock), N.S.W. (mail: P.O. Box 399, Cesnock 2325, N.S.W., Australia)/ Tel. +61 (049) 98-1800

Murwillumbah (New Govardhana)–Tyalgum Rd., Eungella, via Murwillumbah N.S.W. 2484 (mail: P.O. Box 687)/ Tel. +61 (066) 72-1903

RESTAURANTS

Brisbane–Govinda's, 1st floor, 99 Elizabeth St./ Tel. +61 (07) 210-0255

Melbourne–Crossways, 1st floor, 123 Swanston St., Melbourne, Victoria 3000/ Tel. +61 (03) 650 2939

Melbourne–Gopal's, 139 Swanston St., Melbourne, Victoria 3000/ Tel. +61 (03) 650-1578

Perth–Perth - Hare Krishna Food for Life, 200 William St., Northbridge, WA 6003/ Tel. +61 (09) 22716

Sydney–Govinda's Upstairs and Govinda's Take-Away, 112 Darlinghurst Rd., Darlinghurst, N.S.W. 2010/ Tel. +61 (02) 380- 5162

Sydney–Gopal's (at ISKCON Sydney)

NEW ZEALAND AND FIJI

Christchurch, New Zealand–83 Bealey Ave. (mail: P.O. Box 25-190 Christchurch/ Tel. +64 (03) 3665-174

Labasa, Fiji–Delailabasa (mail: Box 133)/ Tel. +679 822912

Lautoka, Fiji–5 Tavewa Ave. (mail: P.O. Box 125)/ Tel. +679 64112

Rakiraki, Fiji–Rewasa, Rakiraki (mail: P.O. Box 94243)

Suva, Fiji–Nasinu 7½ miles (P.O. Box 6376)/ Tel. +679 391-282

Wellington, New Zealand–6 Shotter St., Karori (mail: P.O. Box 2753, Wellington)/ Tel. +64 (04) 764445

RESTAURANTS

Auckland, New Zealand–Gopal's, 1st floor, Civic House, 291 Queen St./ Tel. +64 (09) 3034885

Christchurch, New Zealand–Gopal's, 143 Worcester St./ Tel. +64 (03) 3667-035

Labasa, Fiji–Govinda's, Naseakula Road/ Tel. +679 811364

Lautoka, Fiji–Gopal's, Corner of Yasawa St. and Naviti St./ Tel. +679 62990

Suva, Fiji–Gopal's, 18 Pratt St./ Tel. +679 62990

Suva, Fiji–Gopal's, 37 Cumming St./ Tel. +679 312259

FARM COMMUNITY

Auckland, New Zealand (New Varshan)–Hwy. 18, Riverhead, next to Huapai Golf Course (mail: R.D. 2, Kumeu, Auckland)/ Tel. +64 (09) 4128075

An Introduction to ISKCON and Devotee Life

What is the International Society for Krishna Consciousness?

The International Society for Krishna Consciousness (ISKCON), popularly known as the Hare Kṛṣṇa movement, is a world-wide association of devotees of Kṛṣṇa, the Supreme Personality of Godhead. The same God is known by many names in the various scriptures of the world. In the Bible He is known as Jehovah ("the almighty one"), in the Koran as Allah ("the great one"), and in the *Bhagavad-gītā* as Kṛṣṇa, a Sanskrit name meaning "the all-attractive one".

The movement's main purpose is to promote the well-being of human society by teaching the science of God consciousness (Kṛṣṇa consciousness) according to the timeless Vedic scriptures of India.

The best known of the Vedic texts is the *Bhagavad-gītā* ("Song of God"). It is said to date back 5,000 years to the time when Kṛṣṇa incarnated on earth to teach this sacred message. It is the philosophical basis for the Hare Kṛṣṇa movement and is revered by more than 700 million people today.

This exalted work has been praised by scholars and leaders the world over. M.K. Gandhi said, "When doubts haunt me, when disappointments stare me in the face and I see not one ray of hope, I turn to the *Bhagavad-gītā* and find a verse to comfort me." Ralph Waldo Emerson wrote, "It was the first of books; it was as if an empire spoke to us, nothing small or unworthy, but large, serene, consistent, the voice of an old intelligence which in another age and climate had pondered and thus disposed of the same questions which exercise us." And Henry David Thoreau said, "In the morning I bathe my intellect in the stupendous and cosmogonal philosophy of the *Bhagavad-gītā.*"

Lord Kṛṣṇa teaches in the *Bhagavad-gītā* that we are not these temporary material bodies but are spirit souls, or conscious entities, and that we can find genuine peace and happiness only in spiritual devotion to God. The *Gītā* and other world scriptures recommend that people joyfully chant the holy name of God. Whether one chants His name as Kṛṣṇa, Allah, or Jehovah, one may become blessed with pure love of God.

A Sixteenth-Century Incarnation of Kṛṣṇa

Kṛṣṇa incarnated again in the sixteenth century as Śrī Caitanya Mahāprabhu and popularized the chanting of God's names all over India. He constantly sang these names of God, as prescribed in the Vedic literatures: Hare Kṛṣṇa, Hare Kṛṣṇa, Kṛṣṇa Kṛṣṇa, Hare Hare/ Hare Rāma, Hare Rāma, Rāma Rāma, Hare Hare. The Hare Kṛṣṇa *mantra* is a transcendental sound vibration. It purifies the mind and awakens the dormant love of God in the hearts of all living beings. Lord Caitanya requested His followers to spread this chanting to every town and village of the world.

Anyone can take part in the chanting of Hare Kṛṣṇa and learn the science of spiritual devotion by studying the *Bhagavad-gītā.* This easy and practical process of self-realization will awaken our natural state of peace and happiness.

Many academics and religious leaders who understand the roots of the modern day Hare Kṛṣṇa movement have affirmed the movement's authenticity. Diana L. Eck, professor of comparative religion and Indian studies at Harvard

University, describes the movement as a "tradition that commands a respected place in the religious life of humankind."

Hare Kṛṣṇa Lifestyles

The devotees seen dancing and chanting in the streets, dressed in traditional Indian robes, are, for the most part, full-time students of the Hare Kṛṣṇa movement. The vast majority of followers, however, live and work in the general community, practising Kṛṣṇa consciousness in their homes and attending temples on a regular basis.

There are about 5,000 full-time devotees throughout the world and 200,000 congregational members outside of India. The movement is presently comprised of 267 temples, 40 rural communities, 26 schools, and 45 restaurants in 71 countries. The basic principle of the Hare Kṛṣṇa lifestyle is "simple living and high thinking". A devotee of Kṛṣṇa is encouraged to use his time, energy, talents, and resources in devotional service to God, and not to hanker for selfish ambitions or pleasures which result in frustration and anxiety.

Devotees try to cultivate humanity's inherent spiritual qualities of compassion, truthfulness, cleanliness and austerity. There are four regulative principles which devotees adopt to assist them to develop those qualities and also to help control the insatiable urges of the mind and senses. These are:

1. No eating of meat, fish or eggs.
2. No gambling.
3. No sex other than for procreation within marriage.
4. No intoxication, including all recreational drugs, alcohol, tobacco, tea and coffee.

According to the *Bhagavad-gītā*, indulgence in the above activities disrupts our physical, mental, and spiritual well-being and increases anxiety and conflict in society.

A Philosophy for Everyone

The philosophy of the Hare Kṛṣṇa movement is a nonsectarian monotheistic tradition. It may be summarized in the following eight points:

1. By sincerely cultivating an authentic spiritual science, we can become free from anxiety and achieve a state of pure, unending, blissful consciousness.
2. Each one of us is not the material body but an eternal spirit soul, part and parcel of God (Kṛṣṇa). As such, we are all interrelated through Kṛṣṇa, our common father.
3. Kṛṣṇa is eternal, all-knowing, omnipresent, all-powerful, and all-attractive. He is the seed-giving father of all living beings and the sustaining energy of the universe. He is the source of all incarnations of God.
4. The *Vedas* are the oldest scriptures in the world. The essence of the *Vedas* is found in the *Bhagavad-gītā*, a literal record of Kṛṣṇa's words spoken 5,000 years ago in India. The goal of Vedic knowledge — and of all theistic religions — is to achieve love of God.
5. We can perfectly understand the knowledge of self-realization through the instructions of a genuine spiritual master — one who is free from selfish motives and whose mind is firmly fixed in meditation on Kṛṣṇa.
6. All that we eat should first be offered to Kṛṣṇa with a prayer. In this way Kṛṣṇa accepts the offering and blesses it for our purification.
7. Rather than living in a self-centred way, we should act for the pleasure of Kṛṣṇa. This is known as *bhakti-yoga*, the science of devotional service.
8. The most effective means for achieving God consciousness in this age is to chant the holy names of the Lord: Hare Kṛṣṇa, Hare Kṛṣṇa, Kṛṣṇa Kṛṣṇa, Hare Hare, Hare Rāma, Hare Rāma, Rāma Rāma, Hare Hare.

Kṛṣṇa Consciousness at Home

From what we've read in this book, it is clear how important it is for everyone to practise Kṛṣṇa consciousness, devotional service to Lord Kṛṣṇa. Of course, living in the association of Kṛṣṇa's devotees in a temple or *aśrama* makes it easier to perform devotional service. But if you're determined, you can follow the teachings of Kṛṣṇa consciousness at home and thus convert your home into a temple.

Spiritual life, like material life, means practical activity. The difference is that, whereas we perform material activities for the benefit of ourselves or those we consider ours, we perform spiritual activities for the benefit of Lord Kṛṣṇa, under the guidance of the scriptures and the spiritual master. Kṛṣṇa declares in the *Bhagavad-gītā* that a person can achieve neither happiness nor the supreme destination of life — going back to Godhead, back to Lord Kṛṣṇa — if he or she does not follow the injunctions of the scriptures. How to follow the scriptural rules by engaging in practical service to the Lord is explained by a bona fide spiritual master who is in an authorized chain of disciplic succession coming from Kṛṣṇa Himself.

The timeless practices that are outlined in this book have been taught to us by His Divine Grace A.C. Bhaktivedanta Swami Prabhupāda, the foremost exponent of Kṛṣṇa consciousness in our time.

The purpose of spiritual knowledge is to bring us closer to God, or Kṛṣṇa. Kṛṣṇa says in the *Bhagavad-gītā* (18.55), *bhaktyā mām abhijānāti:* "I can be known only by devotional service." Spiritual knowledge guides us in proper action to satisfy the desires of Kṛṣṇa through practical engagements in His loving service. Without practical application, theoretical knowledge is of little value.

Spiritual knowledge offers direction in all aspects of life.

We should endeavour, therefore, to organize our lives in such a way as to follow Kṛṣṇa's teachings as far as possible. We should try to do our best, to do more than is simply convenient. Then it will be possible for us to rise to the transcendental plane of Kṛṣṇa consciousness, even while living far from a temple.

Chanting Hare Kṛṣṇa

The first principle in devotional service is to chant the Hare Kṛṣṇa *mahā-mantra* (*mahā* means "great"; *mantra* means "sound that liberates the mind from ignorance"):

Hare Kṛṣṇa, Hare Kṛṣṇa, Kṛṣṇa Kṛṣṇa, Hare Hare
Hare Rāma, Hare Rāma, Rāma Rāma, Hare Hare

You can chant these holy names of the Lord anywhere and at any time, but it is best to do it at a specific time of the day. Early morning hours are ideal.

The chanting can be done in two ways: singing the *mantra*, called *kīrtana* (usually done in a group), and saying the *mantra* to oneself, called *japa* (which literally means "to speak softly"). Concentrate on hearing the sound of the holy names. As you chant, pronounce the names clearly and distinctly, addressing Kṛṣṇa in a prayerful mood. When your mind wanders, bring it back to the sound of the Lord's name. Chanting is a prayer to Kṛṣṇa that means "O energy of the Lord (Hare), O all-attractive Lord (Kṛṣṇa), O supreme enjoyer (Rāma), please engage me in Your service." The more attentively and sincerely you chant these names of God, the more spiritual progress you will make.

Because God is all-powerful and all-merciful, He has kindly made it very easy for us to chant His names, and He has also invested all His powers in them. Therefore the names of God and God Himself are identical. This means that when we chant the holy names of Kṛṣṇa and Rāma we are directly associating with God and being purified by such communion. Therefore we should always try to chant with devotion and reverence. The Vedic literature states that Lord Kṛṣṇa is personally dancing on your tongue when you chant His holy name.

When you chant alone, it is best to chant on *japa* beads (available at any of the centres listed in the advertisement at the end of this book). This not only helps you fix your attention on the holy name, but also helps you count the number of times you chant the *mantra* daily. Each strand of *japa* beads contains 108 small beads and one large bead, the head bead. Begin on a bead next to the head bead and gently roll it between the thumb and middle finger of your right hand as you chant the full Hare Kṛṣṇa *mantra.* Then move to the next bead and repeat the process. In this way, chant on each of the 108 beads until you reach the head bead again. This is called one "round" of *japa.* Then, without chanting on the head bead, reverse the beads and start your second round on the last bead you chanted on.

Initiated devotees vow before the spiritual master to chant at least sixteen rounds of the Hare Kṛṣṇa *mantra* daily. But even if you can chant only one round a day, the principle is that once you commit yourself to chanting that round, you should try to complete it every day without fail. When you feel you can chant more, then increase the minimum number of rounds you chant each day — but try not to fall below that number. You can chant more than your fixed number, but you should maintain a set minimum each day. Please note that the beads are sacred and therefore should never touch the ground or be put in an unclean place. To keep your beads clean, it is best to carry them in a special bead bag, also available from any of the temples.

Aside from chanting *japa,* you can also sing the Lord's

holy names in *kīrtana.* Although you can sing *kīrtana* on your own, it is generally performed with others. A melodious *kīrtana* with family or friends is sure to enliven everyone. ISKCON devotees use traditional melodies and instruments, especially in the temple, but you can chant to any melody and use any musical instruments to accompany your chanting. As Lord Caitanya said, "There are no hard and fast rules for chanting Hare Kṛṣṇa." One thing you might want to do, however, is to obtain some *kīrtana* and *japa* audiotapes and hear the various styles of chanting.

Setting Up Your Altar

You will probably find that *japa* and *kīrtana* are more effective when done before an altar. Lord Kṛṣṇa and His pure devotees are so kind that they allow us to worship them even through their pictures. It's something like mailing a letter: You can't mail a letter by placing it in just any box; you must use the postbox authorised by the government. Similarly, we cannot concoct an image of God and worship that, but we may worship the authorised picture of God, and Kṛṣṇa accepts our worship through that picture.

Setting up an altar at home means receiving the Lord and His pure devotees as your most honoured guests. Where should you set up the altar? Well, how would you seat a guest? An ideal place would be clean, well lit, and free from draughts and household disturbances. Your guest, of course, would need a comfortable chair, but for the picture of Kṛṣṇa's form a wall shelf, a mantel-piece, a corner table, or the top shelf of a bookcase will do. You wouldn't seat a guest in your home and then ignore him; you'd provide a place for yourself to sit, too, where you could comfortably face him and enjoy his company, so don't make your altar inaccessible.

What do you need to set up your altar? Here are the essentials:

1. A picture of Śrīla Prabhupāda.
2. A picture of Lord Caitanya and His associates.
3. A picture of Rādhā and Kṛṣṇa.

In addition, you may want an altar cloth, water cups (one for each picture), candles with holders, a special plate for offering food, a small bell, incense, an incense holder, and fresh flowers, which you may offer in vases or simply place before each picture. If you're interested in more elaborate Deity worship, ask any of the ISKCON devotees or write to the Bhaktivedanta Book Trust.

The first person we worship on the altar is the spiritual master. The spiritual master is not God. Only God is God. But because the spiritual master is His dearmost servant, God has empowered him to be His representative and therefore he deserves the same respect as that given to God. The spiritual master links the disciple with God and teaches him the process of *bhakti-yoga.* He is God's ambassador to the material world. When the Queen sends an ambassador to a foreign country, the ambassador receives the same respect as that accorded the Queen, and the ambassador's words are as authoritative as the Queen's. Similarly, we should respect the spiritual master as we would God, and revere his words as we would God's.

There are two main kinds of *guru*: the instructing *guru* and the initiating *guru.* Everyone who takes up the process of *bhakti-yoga* as a result of coming in contact with ISKCON owes an immense debt of gratitude to Śrīla Prabhupāda. Before Śrīla Prabhupāda left India in 1965 to spread Kṛṣṇa consciousness abroad, almost no one outside India knew anything about the practice of pure devotional service to Lord Kṛṣṇa. Therefore, everyone who has learned of the process through his books, his *Back to Godhead* magazine, his tapes, or contact with his followers should offer respect to Śrīla Prabhupāda. As the founder and spiritual guide of the International Society for Krishna Consciousness, he is the prime instructing *guru* of all of us.

Devotees should first of all develop this spiritual understanding and their relationship with Śrīla Prabhupāda. However, the Vedic literature encourages us to become connected to the current link of the chain of spiritual masters. Following Śrīla Prabhupāda's departure, this means accepting initiation from one of Śrīla Prabhupāda's senior followers who are acknowledged as spiritual masters within the movement.

The second picture on your altar should be of the *pañca-tattva*, Lord Caitanya and His four leading associates. Lord Caitanya is the incarnation of God for this age. He is Kṛṣṇa Himself, descended in the form of His own devotee to teach us how to surrender to Him, specifically by chanting His holy names and performing other activities of *bhakti-yoga*. Lord Caitanya is the most merciful incarnation, for He makes it easy for anyone to attain love of God through the chanting of the Hare Kṛṣṇa *mantra*.

And of course, your altar should have a picture of the Supreme Personality of Godhead, Lord Śrī Kṛṣṇa, with His eternal consort, Śrīmatī Rādhārāṇī. Śrīmatī Rādhārāṇī is Kṛṣṇa's spiritual potency. She is devotional service personified, and devotees always take shelter of Her to learn how to serve Kṛṣṇa.

You can arrange the pictures in a triangle, with the picture of Śrīla Prabhupāda on the left, the picture of Lord Caitanya and His associates on the right and the picture of Rādhā and Kṛṣṇa, which, if possible, should be slightly larger than the others, on a small raised platform behind and in the centre.

Or you can hang the picture of Rādhā and Kṛṣṇa on the wall above.

When you establish an altar, you are inviting Kṛṣṇa and His pure devotees to reside as the most important guests in your home. Carefully clean the altar each morning. Cleanliness is essential in the worship of Kṛṣṇa. You would not neglect to clean the room of an important guest. If you have water cups, rinse them out and fill them with fresh water daily. Then place them conveniently close to the pictures. You should remove flowers in vases as soon as they're slightly wilted, or daily if you've offered them at the base of the pictures. You should offer fresh incense at least once a day, and, if possible, light candles and place them near the pictures while you're chanting before the altar.

Please try the things we've suggested so far. It's very simple really: If you try to love God, you'll gradually realize how much He loves you. That's the essence of *bhakti-yoga.*

Prasādam: How to Eat Spiritually

By His omnipotent transcendental energies, Kṛṣṇa can actually convert matter into spirit. If we place an iron rod in a fire, soon the rod becomes red hot and acts just like fire. In the same way, food prepared for and offered to Kṛṣṇa with love and devotion becomes completely spiritualized. Such food is called Kṛṣṇa *prasādam*, which means "the mercy of Lord Kṛṣṇa".

Eating *prasādam* is a fundamental practice of *bhakti-yoga.* In other forms of *yoga* one must artificially repress the senses, but the *bhakti-yogī* can engage his or her senses in a variety of pleasing spiritual activities, such as tasting delicious food offered to Lord Kṛṣṇa. In this way the senses gradually become spiritualised and bring the devotee more and more transcendental pleasure by being engaged in devotional service. Such spiritual pleasure far surpasses any kind of material experience.

Lord Caitanya said of *prasādam*, "Everyone has tasted these foods before. However, now that they have been prepared for Kṛṣṇa and offered to Him with devotion, these foods have acquired extraordinary tastes and uncommon fragrances. Just taste them and see the difference in experience! Apart from the taste, even the fragrance pleases the mind and makes one forget any other aroma. Therefore, it should be understood that the spiritual nectar of Kṛṣṇa's lips must have touched these ordinary foods and imparted to them all their transcendental qualities."

Eating only food offered to Kṛṣṇa is the perfection of vegetarianism. Refraining from animal flesh out of compassion for innocent creatures is certainly a praiseworthy sentiment, but when we go beyond vegetarianism to a diet of *prasādam*, our eating becomes helpful in achieving the goal of human life — reawakening the soul's original relationship with God. In the *Bhagavad-gītā* Lord Kṛṣṇa says that unless one eats only food that has been offered to Him in sacrifice, one will suffer the reactions of *karma*.

How to Prepare and Offer Prasādam

As you walk down the supermarket aisles selecting the foods you will offer to Kṛṣṇa, you need to know what is offerable and what is not. In the *Bhagavad-gītā*, Lord Kṛṣṇa states, "If one offers Me with love and devotion a leaf, a flower, a fruit, or water, I will accept it." Elsewhere, it is explained that we can offer Kṛṣṇa foods prepared from milk products, vegetables, fruits, nuts, and grains. (Write to the Bhaktivedanta Book Trust for one of the many Hare Kṛṣṇa cookbooks.) Meat, fish and eggs are not offerable. A few vegetarian items are also forbidden — garlic and onions, for example, because they tend to agitate the mind, making meditation more difficult. (Hing, asafoetida, is a tasty substitute for them in cooking and is available at most Indian grocers.) Nor can you offer Kṛṣṇa coffee or tea that contain caffeine. If you like these beverages, purchase caffeine-free coffee and herbal teas.

While shopping, be aware that you may find meat, fish, and egg products mixed with other foods; so be sure to read labels carefully. For instance, some brands of yoghurt and sour cream contain gelatin, a substance made from the horns, hooves, and bones of slaughtered animals. Most hard cheese contains rennet, an enzyme extracted from the stomach tissue of slaughtered calves. Look for such cheese labelled as being suitable for vegetarians.

Try to avoid foods cooked by nondevotees. According to the subtle laws of nature the consciousness of the cook affects the food. The principle is the same as that at work in a painting: a painting is not simply a collection of brush strokes on a canvas but an expression of the artist's state of mind, which affects the viewer. So if you eat food cooked by nondevotees such as processed foods etc., then you are likely to absorb a dose of materialism and *karma.* As far as possible in your own cooking use only fresh, natural ingredients.

In preparing food, cleanliness is the most important principle. Nothing impure should be offered to God; so keep your kitchen very clean. Always wash your hands thoroughly before entering the kitchen. While preparing food, do not taste it, for you are cooking the meal not for yourself but for the pleasure of Kṛṣṇa. Arrange portions of the food on dinnerware kept especially for this purpose; no one but the Lord should eat from those dishes. The easiest way to offer food is simply to pray, "My dear Lord Kṛṣṇa, please accept this food," and to chant each of the following prayers three times while ringing a bell.

1. Prayer to Śrīla Prabhupāda:

nama oṁ viṣṇu-pādāya kṛṣṇa-preṣṭhāya bhū-tale
śrīmate bhaktivedānta-svāmin iti nāmine

namas te sārasvate deve gaura-vāṇī-pracāriṇe
nirviśeṣa-śūnyavādi-pāścātya-deśa-tāriṇe

"I offer my respectful obeisances unto His Divine Grace A.C. Bhaktivedanta Swami Prabhupāda, who is very dear to Lord Kṛṣṇa, having taken shelter at His lotus feet. Our respectful obeisances are unto you, O spiritual master, servant of Bhaktisiddhānta Sarasvatī Gosvāmī. You are kindly preaching the message of Lord Caitanyadeva and delivering the Western countries, which are filled with impersonalism and voidism."

2. Prayer to Lord Caitanya:

namo mahā-vadānyāya kṛṣṇa-prema-pradāya te
kṛṣṇāya kṛṣṇa-caitanya-nāmne gaura-tviṣe namaḥ

"O most munificent incarnation! You are Kṛṣṇa Himself appearing as Śrī Kṛṣṇa Caitanya Mahāprabhu. You have assumed the golden colour of Śrīmatī Rādhārāṇī, and You are widely distributing pure love of Kṛṣṇa. We offer our respectful obeisances unto You."

3. Prayer to Lord Kṛṣṇa:

namo brahmaṇya-devāya go-brāhmaṇa-hitāya ca
jagad-dhitāya kṛṣṇāya govindāya namo namaḥ

"I offer my respectful obeisances unto Lord Kṛṣṇa, who is

the worshipable Deity for all *brāhmaṇas*, the well-wisher of the cows and the *brāhmaṇas*, and the benefactor of the whole world. I offer my repeated obeisances to the Personality of Godhead, known as Kṛṣṇa and Govinda."

Remember that the real purpose of preparing and offering food to the Lord is to show your devotion and gratitude to Him. Kṛṣṇa accepts your devotion, not the physical offering itself. God is complete in Himself — He doesn't need anything — but out of His immense kindness He allows us to offer food to Him so that we can develop our love for Him.

After offering the food to the Lord, wait at least five minutes for Him to partake of the preparations. Then you should transfer the food from the special dinnerware and wash the dishes and utensils you used for the offering. Now you, your family and any guests may eat the *prasādam*. While you eat, try to appreciate the spiritual value of the food. Remember that because Kṛṣṇa has accepted it, it is nondifferent from Him, and therefore by eating it you will become purified.

Everything you offer on your altar becomes *prasādam*, the mercy of the Lord. The flowers, the incense, the water, the food having been offered for the Lord's pleasure become spiritualised. The Lord enters into the offerings, and thus the remnants are nondifferent from Him. So you should not only deeply respect the things you've offered, but you should distribute them to others as well. Distribution of *prasādam* is an essential expression of your devotion to Kṛṣṇa.

Everyday Life: The Four Regulative Principles

Anyone serious about progressing in Kṛṣṇa consciousness must try to avoid the following four sinful activities:

1. **Eating meat, fish, or eggs.** These foods are saturated

with the modes of passion and ignorance, and therefore cannot be offered to the Lord. A person who eats these foods participates in a conspiracy of violence against helpless animals and thus curtails his spiritual progress.

2. **Gambling.** Gambling invariably puts one into anxiety and fuels greed, envy, and anger.

3. **The use of intoxicants.** Drugs, alcohol, and tobacco, as well as any drinks or foods containing caffeine, cloud the mind, overstimulate the senses, and make it impossible to understand or follow the principles of *bhakti-yoga.*

4. **Illicit sex.** This is sex outside of marriage or sex in marriage for any purpose other than procreation. Sex for pleasure compels one to identify with the body and prevents from understanding Kṛṣṇa consciousness. The scriptures teach that sex attraction is the most powerful force binding us to the illusions of the material world. Anyone serious about advancing in Kṛṣṇa consciousness should therefore abstain from or regulate sexual activity according to the scriptures. In *Bhagavad-gītā* Kṛṣṇa says that sexual union for conceiving a child to be raised in God consciousness is an act of devotion to Him.

Engagement in Practical Devotional Service

We all must work to earn our livelihood and to maintain home, family, and so on. However, if we try to take the fruits of our labour for ourselves and dependents, we must also accept the karmic reactions incurred because of our work. Kṛṣṇa says in the *Bhagavad-gītā* (3.9), "Work done as a sacrifice for Viṣṇu (Kṛṣṇa) has to be performed. Otherwise work binds one to the material world."

However, it is not necessary to change our occupation, we need to change our attitude. If we are striving for Kṛṣṇa consciousness, if our home has become a temple, and if we share spiritual life with our family members, then what we earn may legitimately be spent for the maintenance of our domestic affairs and the balance engaged in promoting our and others' spiritual lives. Thus, whatever we do we can see it as being part of our devotional service to Kṛṣṇa.

Further, we may also have the opportunity to use our skills and talents directly for Kṛṣṇa. If you're a writer, write for Kṛṣṇa; if you're an artist, create for Kṛṣṇa; if you're a secretary, type for Kṛṣṇa. You may also help a local temple in your spare time, and you could sacrifice some of the fruits of your work by contributing a portion of your earnings to help maintain the temple and propagate Kṛṣṇa consciousness. Some devotees buy Hare Kṛṣṇa literature and distribute it to their friends and associates, or they engage in a variety of services at the temple. There is also a wide network of devotees who gather in each other's homes for chanting, worship, and study. Write to your local temple or the Society's secretary to learn of any such programmes near you.

Additional Devotional Principles

There are many more devotional practices that can help you become Kṛṣṇa conscious. Here are two vital ones:

Studying Hare Kṛṣṇa literature. Śrīla Prabhupāda, the founder-*ācārya* of ISKCON, dedicated much of his time to writing and translating books such as the *Śrīmad-Bhāgavatam.* Hearing the words — or reading the writings — of a realised spiritual master is an essential spiritual practice. So try to set aside some time every day to read Śrīla Prabhupāda's books. You can get a free catalogue of available books and tapes from the Bhaktivedanta Book Trust.

Associating with devotees. Śrīla Prabhupāda established the Hare Kṛṣṇa movement to give people in general the chance to associate with devotees of the Lord. This is the best way to gain faith in the process of Kṛṣṇa consciousness and become enthusiastic in devotional service. Conversely, maintaining intimate connections with nondevotees slows one's spiritual progress. So try to visit the Hare Kṛṣṇa centre nearest you as often as possible.

In Closing

The beauty of Kṛṣṇa consciousness is that you can take as much as you're ready for. Kṛṣṇa Himself promises in the *Bhagavad-gītā* (2.40), "There is no loss or diminution in this endeavour, and even a little advancement on this path protects one from the most fearful type of danger." So bring Kṛṣṇa into your daily life, and we guarantee you'll feel the benefit.

Hare Kṛṣṇa!

STAY IN TOUCH

Now that you've read this book, you may like to further your interest by joining thousands of others as a member of ISKCON.

The International Society for Krishna Consciousness was founded in 1966 by the author of this book, Srila Prabhupada. The Society is dedicated to providing knowledge of Krishna and the science of Krishna consciousness as a means of achieving the highest personal happiness and spiritual fellowship among all living beings. We invite you to join us.

What Does Membership of ISKCON Mean for Me?

For an annual donation of £21 you'll receive a membership package that will keep you fully informed and involved. Here's what you receive (£25 for non UK addresses):

• BACK TO GODHEAD

The Magazine of the Hare Krishna Movement

Each issue of *Back to Godhead* has colorful photos and informative articles on topics such as:

- techniques of *mantra* meditation
- how the spiritual knowledge of the *Vedas* can bring peace, satisfaction, and success in your life
- recipes for a *karma*-free diet
- news of Hare Krishna devotees and devotional projects worldwide
- clear explanations of Vedic science and cosmology
- Krishna conscious perspectives on current affairs... and much more

• THE NAMA HATTA

ISKCON UK's newsletter covering happenings in both UK and Ireland. Articles, letters and lots of news and items of interest.

• VALUABLE DISCOUNTS

All registered members will be sent a valuable 10% Membership Discount Card to use on purchases of books, audio and video tapes, posters, incense, and all other items from UK Hare Krishna shops and the mail order department.

• VAISHNAVA CALENDAR

A beautifully illustrated 12 page wall calendar featuring some of the best of The Bhaktivedanta Book Trust paintings. It will remind you of all the important festivals and celebrations of the Krishna devotee year.

Become a member today and experience the higher taste of *bhakti-yoga.*

Application for Membership

(you can write these details out on a separate piece of paper if you wish)

I wish to be included as a member of ISKCON UK and I have enclosed payment of £21 accordingly for the next years membership. Please send my magazines to:

Surname Mr/Mrs/Ms______________________________

Forenames____________________________________

Address______________________________________

____

Postcode____________________County______________

Please make all payments out to ISKCON:

Signed____________________ Date__________________

PQ

Please Return this application to:
Membership Service Dept., ISKCON,
2 St. James Rd., Watford, WDI 8EA

BHAGAVAD-GITA AS IT IS

The world's most popular edition of a timeless classic.

Throughout the ages, the world's greatest minds have turned to the *Bhagavad-gita* for answers to life's perennial questions. Renowned as the jewel of India's spiritual wisdom, the *Gita* summarizes the profound Vedic knowledge concerning man's essential nature, his environment, and ultimately his relationship with God. With more than fifty million copies sold in twenty languages, *Bhagavad-gita As It Is,* by His Divine Grace A.C. Bhaktivedanta Swami Prabhupada, is the most widely read edition of the *Gita* in the world. It includes the original Sanskrit text, phonetic transliterations, word-for-word meanings, translation, elaborate commentary, and many full-colour illustrations.

	Pocket	Vinyl	Hard	Deluxe
UK	**£3.00**	**£5.25**	**£7.95**	**£13.95**
US	$3.90	$8.50	$10.30	$18.00
AUS		$11.00	$14.00	$28.00

EASY JOURNEY TO OTHER PLANETS

One of Srila Prabhupada's earliest books, *Easy Journey* describes how *bhakti-yoga* enables us to transfer ourselves from the material to the spiritual world.

Softbound, 96 pages

UK: £1.00; US: $1.00; AUS: $2.00

BEYOND BIRTH AND DEATH

What is the self? Can it exist apart from the physical body? If so, what happens to the self at the time of death? What about reincarnation? Liberation? *Beyond Birth and Death* answers these intriguing questions, and more.

Softbound, 96 pages

UK: £1.00; US: $1.00; AUS: $2.00

THE HIGHER TASTE

A Guide to Gourmet Vegetarian Cooking and a Karma-Free Diet

Illustrated profusely with black-and-white drawings and eight full-colour plates, this popular volume contains over 60 tried and tested international recipes, together with the why's and how's of the Krishna conscious vegetarian life-style.

Softbound, 176 pages

UK: £1.00; US: $1.99; AUS: $2.00

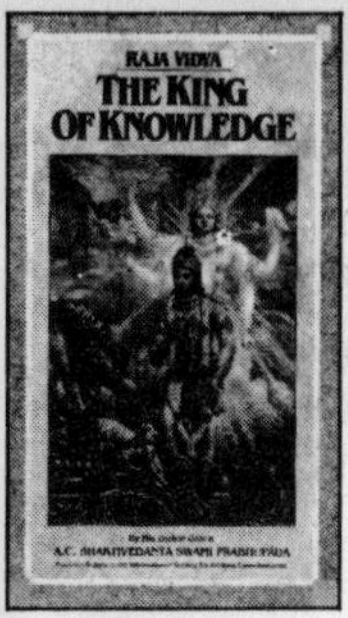

RAJA-VIDYA: THE KING OF KNOWLEDGE

In this book we learn why knowledge of Krishna is absolute and frees the soul from material bondage.

Softbound, 128 pages

UK: £1.00; US: $1.00; AUS: $2.00

THE PERFECTION OF YOGA

A lucid explanation of the psychology, techniques, and purposes of *yoga;* a summary and comparison of the different *yoga* systems; and an introduction to meditation.

Softbound, 96 pages

UK: £1.00; US: $1.00; AUS: $2.00

MESSAGE OF GODHEAD

An excerpt: "The influences of various people, places, and terms have led us to designate ourselves as Hindus, Muslims, Christians, Buddhists, Socialists, Bolsheviks, and so forth. But when we attain transcendental knowledge and are established in *sanatana-dharma,* the actual, eternal religion of the living entity, the spirit soul, then and then only can we attain real, undeniable peace, prosperity, and happiness in this world."

Softbound, 68 pages

UK: £1.00; US: $1.00; AUS: $2.00

GREAT
VEGETARIAN DISHES

Featuring over 100 stunning full-colour photos, this new book is for spiritually aware people who want the exquisite taste of Hare Krishna cooking without a lot of time in the kitchen. The 240 international recipes were tested and refined by world-famous Hare Krishna chef Kurma dasa.

240 recipes, 192 pages, coffee table size hardback

UK: £12.95; US: $19.95; AUS: $24.95

THE HARE KRISHNA BOOK OF
VEGETARIAN COOKING

A colourfully illustrated, practical cookbook that not only helps you prepare authentic Indian dishes at home, but also teaches you about the ancient tradition behind India's world-famous vegetarian cuisine.

130 kitchen-rested recipes, 300 pages hardback

UK: £8.95; US: $11.60; AUS: $15.00

STAY IN TOUCH...

❒ Please send me a free information pack, including the small booklet *Krishna the Reservoir of Pleasure* and a catalogue of available books.

- ❒ Bhagavad-gita As It Is ❒ Pocket ❒ Vinyl ❒ Hard ❒ Deluxe
- ❒ Great Vegetarian Dishes
- ❒ The Hare Krishna Book of Vegetarian Cooking
- ❒ The Higher Taste
- ❒ Raja-Vidya: The King of Knowledge
- ❒ Easy Journey to Other Planets
- ❒ Beyond Birth and Death
- ❒ The Perfection of Yoga
- ❒ Message of Godhead

Please send me the above books. I enclose $/£________ to cover the cost and understand that the prices given include postage and packaging. (All prices offered here are greatly reduced from our normal retail charges!)

Name____

PLEASE PRINT

Address____

____________________________ Postcode________________

PQ

Post this form with payment to:

In Europe: The Bhaktivedanta Book Trust, P.O. Box 324, Borehamwood, Herts, WD6 1NB, U.K.

In North America: The Bhaktivedanta Book Trust, 3764 Watseka Ave., Los Angeles, CA 90034, U.S.A.

In Australasia: The Bhaktivedanta Book Trust, P.O. Box 262, Botany, N.S.W. 2019, Australia